PRAISE FOR HARRY OLDMEADOW'S PREVIOUS BOOKS

Journeys East is the most comprehensive, engaging, and responsible treatment of the advent of Asian thought to the West that has ever been written.

  – Huston Smith

No other available study can compare in either breadth or depth with Oldmeadow's treatment of the very important encounter of the West with the spiritual traditions of the East during the past two centuries.

  – Seyyed Hossein Nasr on *Journeys East*

This is as important a book in the field of the *philosophia perennis* as I have encountered. Oldmeadow has given us a mountain ledge view of the realm of Traditionalism and Perennialism as expounded by its greatest sage, Frithjof Schuon, and he has done so with impeccable scholarship as well as with a stunning breadth of insight that is as spiritually rich as it is intellectually rigorous...

  – Mark Perry, translator of Schuon's works, on *Frithjof Schuon and the Perennial Philosophy*

In an age when matters of the spirit seem like mere vapor...it is necessary to find touchstones — tangible points of contact — in order to make the great spiritual heritage of mankind immediate and real to us again. These penetrating essays serve to do just this.

> – Rodney Blackhirst, author of *Primordial Alchemy*, on *Touchstones of the Spirit*

A wonderful and fascinating book! The definitive introduction to the legacy of Abhishiktananda, the French Benedictine to whom it was given to become a Master of the Vedantic way.

> – Wolfgang Smith, author of *Cosmos and Transcendence*, on *A Christian Pilgrim in India*

This is an extraordinary book. Oldmeadow's groundbreaking interpretation takes Black Elk studies to a profound new level.

> – Wilhelm K. Meya, Director, Lakota Language Consortium, on *Black Elk, Lakota Visionary*

TIMELESS TRUTHS & MODERN DELUSIONS

TIMELESS TRUTHS & MODERN DELUSIONS

*The Perennial Philosophy
as a guide for contemporary Buddhists*

by
HARRY OLDMEADOW

PLATFORM
BOOKSELLERS + PUBLICATIONS

Melbourne & London
2021

Timeless Truths and Modern Delusions

Platform Booksellers + Publications Pty Ltd
209/119 Turner Street Abbotsford, VIC 3067
www.platformbooks.co
info@platformbooks.co

Printed in Australia.

The artwork on the front cover depicts Shakyamuni Buddha in Sambhogakaya form with the Melbourne city skyline and Yarra river in the background. He is displaying the Bhumisparsa 'earth witness' mudra. Bhumisparsa is an Indian earth guardian deity purported to have witnessed Shakyamuni Buddha's enlightenment.

Cover artwork by Adam Parata
Cover design by Matthew Dawson
Photography by Harry Oldmeadow
Transcribed by Jarrah Wishart
Edited by Laura Dainty
Typeset by Stephanie Lightfoot
Proofread by Matthew Dawson

National Library of Australia
Harry Oldmeadow, 1947
Timeless Truths and Modern Delusions: The Perennial Philosophy as a guide for contemporary Buddhists
Printed book ISBN: 978-0-6488830-2-9 (paperback)
Ebook ISBN: 978-0-6488830-3-6

For my brother Peter,
scholar, philosopher and Dharma practitioner.

"Our own time" possesses no quality or criterion of values in regard to that which is timeless. It is the timeless that, by its very nature, is the measure of our time.

– Frithjof Schuon

CONTENTS

PREFACE

I N 2003, at the invitation of Traleg Kyabgon Rinpoche, I gave two talks at E-Vam Institute, presenting a traditionalist perspective on Buddhism and the challenges it faced in the modern world. Traleg Kyabgon was keen to eventually bring the 2003 talks into print, a project which has now come to fruition thanks to the initiatives of Matthew Dawson. In consultation with the author, Matthew also decided to gather together more material which would illuminate the three inter-related subjects which had been the central concern of the talks: the perennial philosophy as espoused by traditionalists such as René Guénon, Ananda Coomaraswamy and Frithjof Schuon, the critique of modernity elaborated by such writers, and the unprecedented situation confronting Buddhism in the modern West. The book can also be located within the over-arching theme of the spiritual meeting of East and West, an encounter which presents serious hazards as well as fertile possibilities. One of the beneficent outcomes of East-West intercourse is the presence of centers such as the E-Vam Institute in Melbourne, established by Traleg Kyabgon Rinpoche, the ninth tulku, or incarnation, of the Traleg Rinpoches of Tibet. Like many other custodians of the Buddhist heritage of Tibet he was deeply engaged with the issues which are canvassed in the following pages. The book is addressed, in the first place, to Western Buddhist practitioners, particularly those not already familiar with the traditionalist writers. More generally it might engage readers who are interested in the epochal but still little understood confluence of the great spiritual traditions of East and West.

Harry Oldmeadow
Bendigo, September 2020

ACKNOWLEDGEMENTS

M Y HEARTFELT thanks go to the E-Vam Institute for the invitation to deliver the two talks which now find their way into print. I am also indebted to Platform Booksellers and Publications and all those who have helped in the preparation and production of this book, especially: Matt Dawson who conceived and nurtured the project, Laura Dainty for her editorial work, Jarrah Wishart for his transcription work, Stephanie Lightfoot for typesetting, and Adam Parata for the artwork.

Due acknowledgement is also made to the organizations and publishers under whose auspices the pieces in this compilation first appeared:

Religion, the Perennial Philosophy, and Traditionalism
An edited transcript of a talk at the Kagyu E-Vam Institute, Carlton, September 2003.

Buddhism and the Spiritual Encounter of East and West
An edited transcript of a talk at the Kagyu E-Vam Institute, Carlton, September 2003.

Looking Forward to Tradition
A talk at Lincoln Hall, London, December 2014, for the Temenos Academy under the auspices of the Matheson Trust. Later

published, with minor modifications, in *The Temenos Academy Review* (London), Vol 18, December 2015.

On Frithjof Schuon's *Treasures of Buddhism*
From the Editor's Preface to Frithjof Schuon's *Treasures of Buddhism* (Bloomington: World Wisdom, 2018).

On Marco Pallis' *The Way and the Mountain*
From the Introduction (Bloomington: World Wisdom, 2008).

Five East-West Bridge-Builders
Chapter 3 of *Journeys East: 20th Century Western Encounters with Eastern Religious Traditions* (Bloomington: World Wisdom, 2004).

Notes on "Spirituality"
First published in the electronic journal *Vincit Omnia Veritas* (France/USA), 1:2, at: http://www.ruh.religioperennis. org/Issue1_2.html; subsequently published in print form in *Vincit Omnia Veritas: Collected Essays*, ed. R. Fabbri & T. Scott (Bendigo: La Trobe University, 2008).

Cosmic Cycles and the Kali Yuga
Chapter 11 of *Frithjof Schuon and the Perennial Philosophy* (Bloomington: World Wisdom, 2010).

To a Buddhist Beat: Allen Ginsberg on Politics, Poetics and Spirituality
Published in *Beyond the Divide* (Bendigo), 2:1, Winter, 1999.

A Few Reflections Provoked by the Current Pandemic

A response to a request from the Editor of *Sacred Web* to provide brief comments on the Covid-19 crisis; written in April 2020, published in *Sacred Web: A Journal of Tradition and Modernity* (Vancouver), Issue 45, June 2020.

Glossary of Eastern Terms

Much of the Glossary is taken from World Wisdom publications, particularly *Treasures of Buddhism.*

EDITOR'S INTRODUCTION

T HIS BOOK project began with transcripts of two talks Harry Oldmeadow gave at E-Vam Institute in September, 2003. When I first read through these transcripts, I was invigorated and uplifted, for here at last, I felt, was an honest, balanced, and comprehensive discussion of tradition and modernity, of tradition within modernity, and of how we might move forward.

In the first of these two talks, "Religion, the Perennial Philosophy, and Traditionalism", Harry gives a presentation of religion, or tradition in general – its constituent elements, its origins, its application, its outer and inner aspects – following the thought of the perennial philosophers. This group of thinkers saw the need to create a platform for inter-religious understanding in light of the globalization that had brought a plethora of the world's traditions into sudden contact. This presentation is illuminating and, moreover, it gives the discussions that follow a proper background and context.

In the second of these talks, "Buddhism and the Spiritual Encounter of East and West", Harry discusses modern science and philosophy, their origins and also their limitations. He shows how they have outstepped their boundaries in becoming the unchecked modern worldview, and the troubling consequences of this. Harry puts science into its context, the context that modern science itself seems to have lost. He then highlights the challenges that modernity poses to religion in general and to Buddhism in particular, and the challenges of transmitting Eastern traditions to the modern West.

To complement and expand on these two talks, we then chose one more talk and seven articles from Harry's many lectures and publications. Harry then supplemented these with a glossary, an excellent resource for readers not yet familiar with Buddhism and other Eastern traditions, and an appendix on the perennialist school, a list of recommended reading, and a bibliography.

In "Looking Forward to Tradition", Harry discusses tradition in light of the understanding of the perennial philosophers, or traditionalists, "a small group of thinkers and writers who have hitherto exerted only a marginal influence on the anglophone world but whose works unravel some of the darkest enigmas of modernity." This discussion of ancient truths and modern delusions is, in many ways, the heart of the entire book.

In "On Frithjof Schuon's *Treasures of Buddhism*", a preface to Schuon's work, Harry summarizes and clarifies many of the misunderstandings of Buddhism that have arisen in modern times. This is followed by "On Marco Pallis' *The Way and the Mountain*", a short article that brings to our attention the writings of Marco Pallis, a Greek-British mountaineer who travelled to Tibet on numerous occasions between 1923 and 1947. Pallis was one of a handful of Westerners to experience the traditional culture of Tibet before it was violated by the Communist invasion of the 1950s and eventually became a Buddhist practitioner himself. When writing about the Buddhist *Vajrayāna*, Pallis drew on the metaphysical presentations of Frithjof Schuon and Ananda Coomaraswamy. He became the most significant Buddhist writer within the perennialist school.

"Five East-West Bridge-Builders" and "To a Buddhist Beat" discuss the personal journeys and contributions of several influential individuals, all followers of tradition, and provide valuable context and perspective with regards to the transmission of traditions from East to West.

"Notes on "Spirituality", a short but pertinent article, looks at the growing popularity of the notion of "spirituality" as separate from "religion", and suggests that any notion of spirituality divorced from the revelations and forms of tradition is a contradiction in terms. "Cosmic Cycles and the Kali Yuga" discusses the doctrine of cycles, pointing out that this cyclical understanding of time pervades *all* traditions, both Eastern and Western, and how, because of their interconnection, the degeneration of mankind is reflected in the outer environment.

The book closes with "A few reflections provoked by the current pandemic", a short article written at the start of the Covid lockdowns. Here Harry highlights once more the connection between our inner condition and our outer environment, a vital and pervasive connection acknowledged and understood by all the traditions of the world. In conclusion, Harry writes, "Do we have the wise humility to ask ourselves, in a spirit of severe seriousness, for what transgressions [of our divine origin and purpose] our current sufferings might be a sanction, and to ponder deeply how we might best meet this test and thereby undergo purification, not only of ourselves but of our darkened world? Without an unsparing self-examination of this kind we may, in one way or another, be doomed."

Such comments might not be easy to digest, but they are becoming increasingly difficult, and increasingly painful, to ignore. With the support of the wisdom contained in these pages, may we all find the humility and courage to embark on such self-examination.

We would like to express our gratitude to Traleg Kyabgon Rinpoche IX for inviting Harry to give the two talks that were the impetus for this project, and to E-Vam Institute for being an avenue for a wealth of dialogue since its founding by Rinpoche in 1982. Most especially, we would like to express our gratitude to Harry for giving us permission to create this book and for sharing his wealth of rare knowledge and courageous insight, the fruit of many years' of deep thought. Finally, and by extension, we would like to pay our respects to all the great traditions of both East and West and to all those who have contributed to their transmission and continuance.

Laura Dainty

RELIGION, THE PERENNIAL PHILOSOPHY AND TRADITIONALISM

The term philosophia perennis...signifies the totality of primordial and universal truths — and therefore of the metaphysical axioms — whose formulation does not belong to any particular system...

– Frithjof Schuon

By directing our gaze toward the perennial wisdom of the traditional worlds, these authors show us that what our world most requires is nothing short of a wholesale reorientation of its outlook, for "as a man thinks, so he becomes".

– Huston Smith

Introduction

A B O U T 30 years ago, I was at home one day reading *The Nation Review.*[1] I was checking out a review of a Grateful Dead record when my eyes wandered down the page to a book review. The book sounded rather interesting, so I went out and bought a copy. It was astonishing, the most startling book I'd read hitherto. It was quite unlike anything I'd ever read before and it just knocked me out. The book was *The Sword of Gnosis*[2] edited by Jacob Needleman, a collection of essays by a group of writers who all subscribed to the same general philosophy, although they belonged to different religious traditions. This compilation was concerned with religion, cosmology, metaphysics and sacred art, and all manner of related subjects, but there were various shared themes and motifs that ran through the collection. After this, I quickly started accumulating works by the authors represented in this anthology. They did not give themselves any particular name or description, but the term they came to be known by is "traditionalists" or, alternatively, "perennialists". It is about their work that I want to talk tonight. Who are these people? There are a good few of them by now, but the three pre-eminent figures are the French writer René Guénon, the Anglo-Ceylonese Ananda Coomaraswamy, and Frithjof Schuon, a Swiss-German.

What Constitutes Religion?

Before I talk about these people and their works, I would like briefly to define what I understand by the term "religion" in general. I see all religions as having the following seven elements: myths, doctrines, values, sacred art, rituals, institutions, and adherents.

The first element that is crucial for religion in my view is myth. Now, myths don't have a very good reputation these days. In fact, "myth" has become a rather pejorative term. When people say that something's mythical, what do they mean? They mean it's unreal, a fabrication, a childish story, a fantasy, an illusion. But, of course, I'm not using the word that way but in its proper sense, which is to say a story or narrative, often allegorical, that embodies fundamental truths which are difficult to express in any other way. As far as I can see, all religious traditions have myths.

Secondly, we need doctrines. What are these doctrines about? Well, to cut a long story short, they are about the nature of reality. It seems to me that one *sine qua non* of religion is that it has to give an account of reality. All religions take it for granted that there is a reality greater than the world of the senses, greater than the material, empirical world that we can see around us. They believe that there is something beyond the time-space continuum that is not accessible to sensory apprehension. We can give this other reality various names. The most neutral name I can think of, without privileging any particular religious tradition, is the Absolute, a transcendent reality which is variously described as immutable, outside time and space, and so on and so forth. The world, the life, the reality that can be apprehended by our senses is only relatively real. Therefore, a religion must have a doctrine that gives us an account of both the Absolute and the relative, and of the relationship between the two.

Thirdly, a religion must affirm values, usually enshrined in a moral code. It must privilege certain ideals above others; it must discriminate between good and evil, right and wrong, between behaviour which is appropriate and inappropriate; you can use whichever terms you prefer.

To just run quickly through the next three elements, a religion must also have sacred art, rituals, and formally organized institutions. These are present in all traditions. Finally, to state the obvious, a living religion must have adherents. We might add an eighth element: since these elements that together comprise a religion move through time, each religion also has a history.

This is just my own schema; there are any number of different ways in which people have tried to characterize what constitutes a religion. This is simply my own attempt. We could say that the first two of these seven elements — myths and doctrines refer to *understanding* the world, understanding reality, understanding life. They concern the mode of perception, how we make some sense of reality. The next two elements, values and sacred art, also shape our understanding as well as forming a bridge to our *way of being* in the world which will be informed by our ritual life. Religious institutions provide a framework for the preservation of these various elements and for the ongoing spiritual life of the adherents.

If you want to condense all these constituents of religion into a very simple twofold definition, you can, I think, reduce them all to *doctrine* and *method*. In the case of Buddhism, at the most basic level, we could say that the Four Noble Truths are the foundation of the doctrine and the Eightfold Path is the foundation of the method.

The Traditionalists

Thus far a general understanding of religion. What I now want to talk about more particularly, however, is the traditionalist understanding. To begin with, let me tell you a little about the three figures I mentioned above.

René Guénon was born in 1886 and died in 1951. He spent the first forty-four years of his life in France before moving to Egypt where he became a Muslim and was initiated into a Sufi order. He lived a life of great obscurity in Egypt, but all the while he wrote books. From among his many works, two of the most important are *The Crisis of the Modern World* which he wrote in the 1920s, and his masterwork, *The Reign of Quantity and the Signs of the Times*, published in 1945. He was a somewhat controversial thinker and has attracted all manner of disciples, some of whom are a bit off the wall. For instance, if you google René Guénon all sorts of bizarre things will come up. So, if you are interested in Guénon my suggestion would be to read his actual works and to take anything his so-called followers say with a pinch of salt; some of these "followers" should be approached with a great deal of caution.

Guénon's work itself is quite extraordinary. *The Reign of Quantity*, a book that is not very well known and was out of print for many years, is, to my mind, the most extraordinary book of the 20th century and one of the most important. It is not altogether surprising that it is a neglected work. Why? Because it is completely at odds with almost everything that we in the modern world take for granted. A more devastating assault on the ideas and values of modernity would be hard to come across; it is a frightening book. The first time I read it I was profoundly disturbed. It's a chilling book in many ways and its author strikes some readers as a rather remote and cold figure (quite different, apparently, from how he was in real-life). A lot of people cannot cope with *The Reign of Quantity*. They read three or four pages and then declare the author to be a madman. It *is* a very challenging book. What is the book actually about? In short, it is an affirmation of tradition and a repudiation of modernity. I will discuss what we mean by the word tradition and modernity in a few moments.

Guénon was primarily interested in metaphysics, which is to say that he was interested in the way in which the various traditions, particularly in their esoteric aspects, described reality. He defines metaphysics as the "science of the Real", and by the "Real" he does not, of course, mean the material world. Guénon shared with the Hindus, and indeed with most religious doctrines, the view that the material world is only relatively real, and that there is a "more real" world lying behind, so to speak, the material world. More about Guénon later.

Ananda Coomaraswamy

Coomaraswamy was born in 1877 to an English mother and a Sri Lankan father; he died in 1947. He spent his childhood in England and trained as a geologist. He then went back to Sri Lanka to carry out a geological survey. While he was in the hinterland of Sri Lanka, traveling from village to village, he was captivated by the traditional crafts of the village folk. Soon afterwards he abandoned geology and, in a very short period of time, became an authority on traditional Asian arts and crafts. He eventually became the curator of the Boston Museum which houses one of the largest and most impressive collections of Asian art in the Western world. When Coomaraswamy came across Guénon's works he was deeply impressed by them and came to share the same general philosophy, a direction in which his own researches were already leading him.

Schuon belonged to the next generation. He was born in 1907 and died only recently, in 1998. While I said that Guénon's *The Reign of Quantity* is the most extraordinary book of the twentieth century, Frithjof Schuon, when we consider his work as a whole, is the most significant thinker and writer of our era. Such is my view. He wrote more than 30 books; one which might be of particular interest to you is *The Treasures of Buddhism*.[3]

Schuon, like Guénon, began his career in design. He was particularly interested in the design of fabrics. Nevertheless, he too found his way to North Africa, where, in Algeria, he became a disciple of the Sufi Sheikh, Ahmad Al-Alawi (1869-1934), and a member of his Sufi order, the Alawiyya. Eventually Schuon became the head of that order. Later he moved back to Switzerland. He lived there for a good many years until the early 1980s when he moved to the United States where he passed his last years. He was a prolific writer and, in my opinion, he gave the most formidable, the most beautiful, the most exhaustive and the most profound exposition of what is often called the perennial philosophy.

THE PERENNIAL PHILOSOPHY
The Traditionalists' View

All three of these figures were exponents of the *philosophia perennis*, the timeless Wisdom of the Ages. You may have come across this term before. The most likely place in which you would have encountered it is Aldous Huxley's famous book, *The Perennial Philosophy*, published in 1945. This book caused a huge amount of excitement. Huxley's principal thesis in this book is simple: all of the major religious traditions are, in their core teachings, essentially the same. He claimed that as far as their accounts of reality and their various doctrines are concerned, they are essentially the same and only accidentally different. To demonstrate this fact, he chose about twenty themes and then looked at various scriptures from the different traditions, pilfered passages from here and there, pasted them all together, and said, "look, they're all talking about the same thing". However, the problem with Huxley's exposition of the perennial philosophy, from the traditionalist point of view, is that he made one fatal error. This was to believe that we can identify and distil the essence of these different religions, and separate it from the religious forms through which it has been transmitted over the centuries. In this way, Huxley is seeking a kind of super-religion, a universal religion, which takes the best from each religion, melding together what he describes as "the common denominators" (an awful term to describe religious doctrines!). Having combined these "common denominators" together, he then asserts that this is what religion is all about. He proposes that we forget the differences between the various traditions, that we abandon their forms as so many incidental accretions, and that we commit ourselves to this common essence.

Of course, there have been plenty of others who have made proposals of this kind. For instance, some of the Neo-Hindus in India, such as Vivekananda, were keen on this sort of approach. Vivekananda was probably the best known Indian Swami (teacher) in the Western world in the late nineteenth century. He caused a huge commotion at the Parliament of the World Religions in Chicago in 1893 with his charming and articulate manner, his charismatic personality, even though, ironically, he hadn't been officially invited and just turned up! In any case, he too had ideas similar to those of Huxley.

Part of the problem with the position that was held by Huxley and Vivekananda and many others is that they fall captive to one of the most pernicious of modern prejudices, and that is the notion of progress. Namely, the idea that humankind is evolving, that we are becoming smarter, that we are coming to understand more about reality, and that we can somehow improve upon the teachings of the past, as if the teachings of Lord Buddha could be improved upon — as if! The idea is preposterous, is it not? Vivekananda says in one of his works that the teachings of the Buddha, of Lao Tze, of Jesus, and of Mohammad were all very well in their day, the implication being that their day is over and that we now have to move on to something higher.

Nothing could be further removed from the spirit of the traditionalists. They too believe that there is a common basis to all the religions, they too believe that there is a kind of common essence, if you wish to use that term, shared by all the different religious traditions. However, the crucial point is that they do not propose extracting it from the forms — doctrines, myths, ethical codes, rituals, scriptures and the like — which contain it. So, they take precisely the opposite attitude to religious forms to that taken by people like Huxley. They regard the religious forms as precious and believe that they must be preserved at all costs, for without the forms there can be no understanding, no wisdom, and no living tradition. There can only be syncretism, a kind of 'spiritual Esperanto', as Coomaraswamy put it, which has as much chance of success as Esperanto had! This is the position of the perennial philosophers I am discussing, as distinguished from other so-called perennial philosophers like Huxley and Vivekananda.

Let us first consider the question of origins. From the perennial philosopher's point of view, all religions and traditions are of supra-human origin. The kind of accounts that are given by cultural historians and anthropologists simply will not do. No, they will not do! Religion is not a cultural construction. That is not to say, of course, that a religious tradition doesn't bear the imprint of the culture in which it appears. Of course it does. Regarding this, T.S. Eliot correctly articulated the relationship in his book *Notes Towards the Definition of Culture* in which he said that culture, properly speaking, is the embodiment or incarnation of religion. What is a properly constituted culture? It is the application of religion to all domains of life; that is what a culture really is. We, on the other hand, seem to have things upside down, because we imagine that culture is something broader than religion and that religion is a part of culture. This is getting the state of affairs upside down and inside out. Religion, or tradition – these two terms being more or less synonymous from this point of view – is something larger than culture. Its origins are supra-human; it is not of human contrivance. Religions do not appear under the pressure of human initiative or human invention. I understand that this point of view might be difficult for some Buddhists to accept, especially Theravadin Buddhists. I imagine that Mahayana Buddhists will have less of a problem with this kind of notion. Nevertheless, it is only to be expected that there will be some resistance to this particular idea from some schools of Buddhism.

All religions derive from a Revelation – all integral religions, which is to say all religious traditions that are pre-modern. What do we mean by modern? Well, as far as the Western world goes, the modern era began at the end of the Middle Ages. The medieval world was the last fully traditional European culture. As far as the perennialists are concerned, it has been a downhill slope in the West ever since the end of the Middle Ages. Why? Because the story of the last five or six hundred years traces the gradual triumph of a worldview which is profoundly antithetical and often hostile to religion. This is one of the reasons why the traditionalists are not very popular, why people find them challenging and difficult to read, and why a lot of people just reject them out of hand. The perennialists have no truck with modernity and regard any compromise with the ideologies of modernity as spiritual suicide.

We are talking at present about origins and arguing that all traditions derive from another reality. That is their origin. You can conceptualize, describe and label this other reality in all manner of different ways. You can call it God, Allah, Brahman, the Tao, Nirvana or *Shūnyata* (emptiness). Like the Lakota you can call it *Wakan-Tanka*. Call it what you will but, needless to say, in all traditions there is an affirmation of this other Reality, one which is both "beyond" (transcendent) and "within" (immanent). As I observed earlier, this is somewhat problematic in Buddhism which at times takes an apophatic or negative attitude towards metaphysical formulations. The Buddha himself refused to answer the "indeterminant questions".[4] Buddhism is generally reluctant to make affirmations about this other reality, but nevertheless it is there. It does at times become explicit in the Buddhist scriptures, such as in the Sutra passage where the Buddha says, to paraphrase, that there is the incomposite, impartite, and unchanging, without which there would be no possibility of liberation. The Buddha characteristically describes this other reality in negative terms — not composed, without parts, without change. He states that, if it were not for this unchanging reality which lies beyond this ephemeral world of constant flux and of multiplicity, liberation would not be possible. In this way, we can see that, although Buddhism comes at it from a different angle and although on the face of it there might seem to be some problems, Buddhism does affirm this greater reality from whence religion came.

To reiterate, the origin of religions is supra-human, and at the moment of a tradition's appearance in time and space, its entry into the world of flux, the religion is in its purest form. This is why Vivekananda's assertion that we can improve on the teachings of the Buddha must be thrown out of court. As far as the Buddhist tradition is concerned, there can be nothing more profound, nothing more beautiful, nothing more sacred than the moment of the tradition's origin in the person, life, and teachings of the Buddha himself. Likewise with all other traditions.

Sometimes we cannot locate the point of origin historically, but this does not matter. We cannot, for instance, pinpoint when the tradition of the Indigenous Australians began, but we do know that they have been here for tens of thousands of years and that their tradition stretches far back into the mists of time. Similarly with the Chinese. We do not know when their tradition began. On the other hand, with some other traditions it is very clear. We can identify a historical figure, a book, or an event as the starting point. Regardless of whether it can be pinpointed historically or not, it is as if, through an opening in the barrier between Heaven and Earth, a kind of spiritual charge is released into the world. Whatever metaphor we use will be inadequate, but we can say that a kind of spiritual current flows from the Absolute into the time-space world of relativities.

What does a tradition or a religion do through all of its formal elements? It provides a channel through which that force can be transmitted through time, so that others can access it, can tap into it, so to speak. Hence in each tradition, there is a great deal of emphasis on the notion of transmission, and the Buddhists are very big on this. As you know, in order to be a properly credentialed and reputable Buddhist teacher, for example, it is extremely important to be able to trace your lineage back through a succession of teachers stretching back over a long period of time. There are all sorts of manifestations of this idea of lineages in Tibetan Buddhism, not least in the institution of the Dalai Lama.

Thus, the initial Revelation gives us the wherewithal for the ensuing doctrine and method. Everything needful is already there from the beginning. Somebody might then say, well, how is it then that there weren't any cathedrals in early Christianity, for example? Were the cathedrals an addition to the religion? In a certain sense, yes, but in another sense, no; it actually works the other way around. This is to say that, as time goes by and we grow more and more distant from the origin, the greater the danger that the teaching and our receptivity to the spiritual charge itself becomes weakened. As a result, we need all sorts of new ways of re-expressing it, reviving it, preserving it. We need to meet all sorts of needs which were not present at the time of origin, but which have arisen over the course of time through forgetfulness, through the corruption of the doctrine, through the occurrence of abuses and so on. The reason the early Christians didn't have cathedrals is because they didn't need them. The cathedral came into being to fulfill certain changing needs of the people in later times.

Time: The Doctrine of Cycles

From this discussion, another prominent idea held by the traditionalists is beginning to emerge, an idea that is completely contrary to the modern mentality. It is a kind of counter-evolutionary view. In other words, they assert that there are no grounds for supposing that things are getting better, and there are good grounds for supposing that, in fact, things are getting worse. Perhaps thinking of things in terms of "better and worse" itself proves to be inadequate in the end and we should try to move beyond thinking about the situation in those terms. Nevertheless, if we must think in terms of things getting better or worse, all the evidence indicates that things are deteriorating. Inevitably someone will protest against this statement and say, "But we got rid of slavery! What about the fact that we don't have Inquisitions anymore? What of the many improvements we have seen in modern times? What of scientific and medical discoveries?" All of these changes, no doubt, may be good in themselves, but they are not real improvements in the overall situation; they are, it might be said, compensations. When we look at the picture overall, we may see that they are no more than compensations for all of the other things that have been lost and destroyed by modernity.

If we stand back and take a calm, dispassionate look, is the notion that the modern age is an improvement not the most implausible of ideas? Let us cast our minds over the 20th century. Have we ever seen a period of more hideous destruction, of more widespread violence, of alienation, of genocide, of confusion, of rampant materialism? Has there ever been an unhappier and more destructive period in human history? I myself do not think so. We are busy making the planet uninhabitable, creating disasters of all manner and kind, and the suicide rates are steadily rising. Is it not suggestive that the highest suicide rates are in the materially most advanced countries? You don't have high suicide rates in India; you have them in Scandinavia, in Western

Europe, in Australia, and the United States. Why? Well, you know the answer. The answer is that people cannot live without meaning, and that is what they face in the modern world. People painfully discover that all the substitutes, all the palliatives, all the alternatives to real spiritual nourishment which would give them a meaningful life, turn to ashes in the hand. They are not worth anything. People wake up to this sooner or later and the result is an overwhelming despair.

To reiterate, the traditionalist view is a counter-evolutionary view, taken largely from the Hindu doctrines which describe time as a cycle of four great ages. According to this doctrine, we are now living in the Kali Yuga, the Iron Age. This is a degenerate time during which life becomes increasingly materialized, increasingly heavy, and genuine spiritual teachings are threatened on all sides. It is a period that is heading towards an endgame. From among the three writers I have mentioned, it is Guénon in particular who takes up this theme.

The Age of Revelations is Over

Another important point in the traditionalist view is that the age of Revelations is long since over. It finished with the Quran, and there can be no more revelations. Among the traditionalists, there are many variations to this point of view and many arguments connected with it, but I will not delve into those here. In short, they all agree that the age of Revelations is over and that the evidence for this lies in the Revelations themselves. When Mohammad declared, "I am the seal of the prophets" it meant just that, that he was the final figure in the succession of prophets. Therefore, from this point of view, there can be no new religions. Anything which claims to be a new religion, to have a new divine dispensation and the like, from this point of view, is a counterfeit, an imposture, a symptom of confusion; it is not the real thing.

EXOTERIC AND ESOTERIC: THE TWO DIMENSIONS OF RELIGION
The Exoteric Dimension

Religion always has two dimensions, so to speak: the exoteric, which is the formal, outer dimension, and the esoteric, which is the inner, secret dimension. The formal dimension is the outer, visible aspect of religion, comprised of its scriptures, rituals, temples, sacred art and so forth. We find these formal elements in all of the religions and it is these elements which give the religion its personality, its character, its distinctive flavor. As Schuon put it, each religion has its own spiritual aroma, its own unique character. Some people have tried to sum up each religion with just one or two words. This is difficult, and of course it is a gross oversimplification, but nevertheless it might be said that the essence of Islam is piety, the remembrance of God at all times. Likewise, it might be said that the essence of Christianity is love, that the essence of Judaism is righteousness, that the essence of Buddhism is wisdom-compassion. As you will be well aware, in Buddhism wisdom and compassion are not two separate things. Rather they are two sides of the same thing: compassion is the dynamic aspect of wisdom, and compassion that is devoid of wisdom is not compassion it all. It is mere sentimentality or sympathy. Similarly with wisdom: genuine wisdom devoid of compassion is simply not possible.

The traditionalists call these formal, visible, outer aspects of religion the exoteric aspect, and as far as most followers are concerned, it comprises the entire religion. The average devotee believes that the exoteric domain itself is what religion is all about and that is how they practice. They perform their duties, they carry out their devotions, they do whatever is needful according to their particular tradition. In the case of a Muslim, for example, the five pillars of Islam – pilgrimage, prayer, offering alms, fasting, and professing faith – are the sum total of their religious practice. That's the entire story as far as most devotees are concerned, and likewise for all other religions.

Moreover, most devotees will believe that their tradition is the best tradition. Sometimes they will go further than that and claim that their tradition is the only valid tradition. From a certain point of view, such a belief is defensible, for it is the nature of things that adherents should think that their tradition is the best tradition. That, after all, is why they belong to it. We must not overemphasize the virtue of tolerance and open-mindedness, because such attitudes are very easy for most of us in the modern world, that is to say for people who believe in nothing. As Schuon says in one of his works, the Christians and Muslims fighting one other in the Crusades were much closer together than either of them are to the modern-day Professor of Comparative Religion who professes tolerance for all religions but believes in none. From this point of view, such fervent commitment to one's own religion, even if it has some unfortunate results, is understandable and defensible, up to a point.

The real problem is that we are now living in a very different world. In the traditional world, for instance in Tibet 500 years ago, Islam, Christianity, Taoism, Judaism, and other religions would have had nothing to do with your own world. You might be dimly aware that there are other people in other parts of the world who have different beliefs and practices, who have different cultures from yours, but most likely you wouldn't be aware of them at all. Of course, that is not the world we live in, one where all cultures, beliefs, and traditions are colliding and everybody is aware of everything. We live in the Global Village and through the internet and the like we can know what's happening in all corners of the world simultaneously. As a result, the world's various religions have all come together, and so attitudes that in the past might have been more or less legitimate are now dangerous and destructive. Such attitudes need to be countered and that is one of the purposes of the traditionalists. I will discuss this in more detail in the next talk concerning "Buddhism and the Spiritual Encounter of the East and West".

The Esoteric Dimension

Each religion has this outer exoteric dimension, but it also has an inner, secret dimension, which is the esoteric. Without the esoteric dimension, the formal, exoteric framework would be worth nothing; it would just be an empty shell. It would be like a body without a heart, and the heart of each religious tradition is rooted in mystical experience. From a Buddhist point of view, the experience of enlightenment is the heart that keeps the whole thing alive. Without it, all of the formal elements, the exoteric structure, would fall down, lifeless.

To help illustrate the traditionalist point of view, I have created a diagram. It is by no means perfect, but it shows how the esoteric dimensions of religions converge. Around the circumference of the diagram are situated the different religions in their exoteric form. One of the inadequacies of this diagram is that the primal traditions – I am referring to the Indigenous Peoples, the Indigenous Americans, the Inuit, the San People of South Africa, and so on – are put on the same footing as the historical religions of Judaism, Christianity, Islam, Buddhism and so forth. It would be better if the primal religions formed an inner ring inside the historical religions, suggesting that, in a certain sense, they are closer to the Absolute than historical religions. That is certainly how Guénon understands it and also how I personally understand it. Moreover, the fact that these primal traditions don't have many of the formal elements which we find in historical religions is not because they were ignorant or superstitious, but because they didn't need them. That is to say, they were living in a state of spiritual awareness and without the impediments of the modern world. To return to the diagram: in the center we have the Absolute, which relates to the esoteric. Arrows come out from the Absolute to the various traditions, the segments around the circle, indicating that they all come from the same place. That's the first point illustrated by the diagram.

The exoteric majority, namely the ordinary followers, more or less remain inside their respective segment, "inside" the formal elements of their tradition. However, within each tradition there are a certain number of people who are capable of the most profound insight and, from the Buddhist point of view, are actually and presently capable of Enlightenment. We could call this group of people, who are necessarily a minority, the spiritual elite, although such an idea sometimes proves offensive to the modern mentality which wants to be egalitarian at all possible costs. Of course, we know that everyone is potentially capable of Enlightenment, so there is spiritual equality in that sense. Nevertheless, we also know that, as far as most of us are concerned, it is going to take us many, many lifetimes to reach Enlightenment. We are in such a confused and ignorant state, so held back by our attachments, that it is going to be a long and arduous journey. All that most of us can hope to do is put one foot forward at a time and hope that we are moving in the right direction.

The esoteric sensibility is able to penetrate the forms, to see through the forms, and see that each religious tradition is but one expression of the truth, one expression amongst many different possible expressions. An image that Schuon used in this regard is geometric figures. There can be all manner of geometric figures – triangles, circles, squares, rhomboids, parallelograms and so on – and it would be absurd to imagine that there could be only one geometric figure. But, the basic principle of all geometric figures is the same.

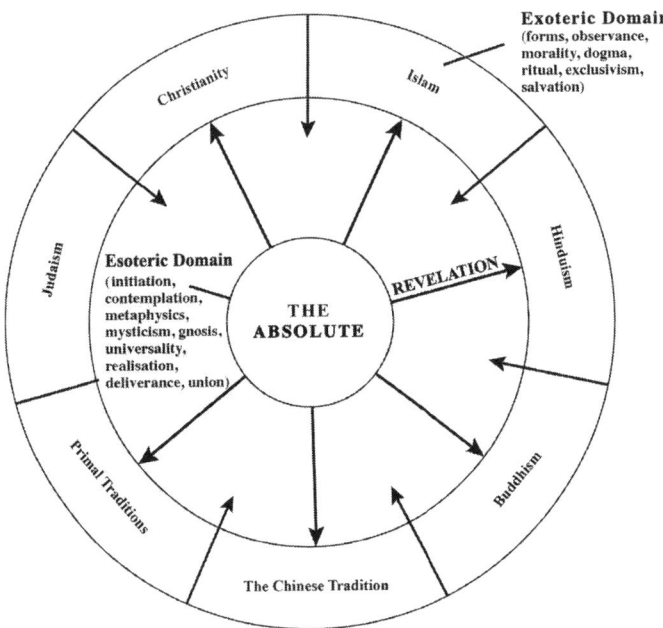

Figure 1 The Exoteric and Esoteric Domains

All religious traditions are a kind of spiritual language and to follow a tradition is like speaking a language. Who would be foolish enough to try to speak Swahili and French and Japanese simultaneously? It cannot be done; you'll just end up talking gobbledygook. The thing to do is to know one language and to speak it as well as you can. (And if you know several languages, all to the good, but you only speak one at a time and you have a special relation to your native language.) Similarly with the traditions: commit yourself to one tradition, adhere to it, follow its methods, believe its doctrines, immerse yourself in that tradition. This is the best that the ordinary adherent can do, and should do.

Only a small minority will be able to see *through* the forms to the truth unqualified, i.e. the center of the circle. Let us imagine the mystics, the sages, the contemplatives, the recluses, the bodhisattvas travelling, so to speak, from this outer circumference towards the Center. What happens when they get to the Center? They are all at the same point. Does it matter from whence they came? Is the person who came from this side of the circle to be granted precedence over the person who came from the other side of the circle? Of course not. Once one is at the Center, the exoteric world, the world of forms, is left behind. But it would be the gravest mistake to say, as Huxley and company do, let's throw the forms away. That is the worst of all possible errors, for it is only through the forms that we can go inwards towards the esoteric, towards the Absolute.

Each Religion Fulfills a Need

The traditionalists believe that each religion is addressed to a particular portion of humanity, a human collectivity with a certain spiritual temperament, so to speak, a certain spiritual receptivity to which that particular religion is addressed. As one of the traditionalists, Seyyed Hossein Nasr, has affirmed, "every revealed religion is *the* religion and *a* religion: *the* religion in that it contains within itself the truth and the means of attaining the truth, and *a* religion since it emphasizes a particular aspect of truth, in conformity with the spiritual and psychological needs of the humanity for whom it is destined".[5] It therefore follows, if this is true, that there can be no question of one religion ever taking over. Of course, it is possible for people to attach themselves to an alien religion, a religion other than the one they were born into. There is no problem with that. However, there can be no question of Europeans at large becoming Buddhists, for instance, just as there can be no question of Tibetans at large becoming Christians. A few might, but they are the exception that proves the rule.

THE CHALLENGES OF THE MODERN WORLD

If we take the traditionalist point of view seriously, it provides us with a basis for fulfilling what, I believe, is the most imperative need in the modern world. The difficulty we face in the modern world is that on the one side we have religion and tradition, or the remnants thereof, and on the other side we have modernity. With modernity, we have science, progress, democracy, freedom, equality, "self-realization" and so on. What we need, in terms of religion and traditions, is a basis for recognizing their convergences and what Schuon has called their "transcendent unity". We need a platform on which we can construct an understanding of religion and tradition that enables all of the different religions to form a common front. By that, I do not in any way mean abandon their traditions and form some wishy-washy "super religion". Not at all. But, we need to recognize that the pertinent issue for the modern world is the issue between tradition on one side and modernity on the other.

Modernity is well on the way to triumphing over tradition. It seems that it's most of the way there already and who knows whether there's any turning back. Nevertheless, we have to try. The surest way to ensure the triumph of modernity and the surest way to guarantee the collapse of tradition is for the religions to fight each other. This, we know, is what is happening in many different parts of the world. Fortunately, the Buddhists have a far better record on this front than most other religions. It is, in fact, the Western monotheistic religions that have gone grotesquely in the other direction, away from the idea of inter-religious harmony. We need an inter-religious concord that is not just based on platitudes, not just based on sentiment, but has a rigorous, intellectual, philosophical basis. This is the kind of antidote we need if we are to free ourselves from all of the worst superstitions of the modern world, and this is what I believe the traditionalist account of religions actually provides.

We like to talk in derogatory tones about the "superstitions" of the people of the past, such as the Indigenous Australians, the people of Ancient India or China, or the Native Americans. We might regard some of their stories as colorful, quaint, and interesting, and think that they did the best they could with what they had. We modern folk, however, we know what's for real. We are grown-up people with our feet on the ground. What do we mean when we say that? We usually mean that we have succumbed to the worldview of modern science, a worldview in which the real is the material. We mean that we have surrendered to all of these pseudo-dogmas, these pernicious anti-traditional ideas, such as the notion of progress and, of course, evolution. In both its biological guise and its social guise, the notion of evolution is absolutely pervasive in modern times. It contaminates almost everything we think about. Scratch almost anybody and you'll find evolutionism in some guise just under the skin there. This has got to be rooted out! But this is too large and complex subject to embark on here so I now invite your thoughts and questions.

✳

QUESTION: Why do some religious traditions replace or "supersede" others?

HARRY OLDMEADOW: That is an interesting question. From the traditionalist point of view, a religion will only take over, as Buddhism did in Tibet, where there is some inadequacy or corruption, at that particular historical moment, in the anterior tradition. What actually happened in Tibet was that the old Bönpo religion was not destroyed but assimilated into the Buddhist perspective. This is one reason why Tibetan Buddhism has its own very particular character. In other cases, it was a matter of the existing religion becoming so decadent and corrupt that it became providential that it should be swept away. An example of this is Roman Paganism. By the time Christianity came along, what had once been a vibrant tradition, tracing its roots back to the Greeks and right back to Homeric times, lay in a complete mess, for the Roman Pagans had fallen into idolatry, the terrible mistake of taking the symbol to be the thing itself. Therefore, it was providential that the remnants of that tradition should be swept aside. But even in this some of the integral elements of the antecedent tradition (Graeco-Roman paganism) were absorbed into the emergent tradition (Christianity), fertilizing it, so to speak, from within.

Q: In simple terms, is the message of the traditionalists that we should endeavor to reach the Absolute by pursuing the heart of the tradition that we choose?

HO: Yes, that is their message, but in pursuing the tradition there can be no by-passing of its forms. Unlike Huxley and thinkers of that ilk, the perennialists are saying that, if you want to reach the center, to continue with the metaphor I've used in the diagram, you need to practice your religion, whatever it may be, to the best of your ability. If you do that, you will travel the furthest distance towards the center of which you, as an individual in this lifetime, are capable. As I was saying before, some of us won't get very far, while others will get a lot further.

An image that Schuon and the others often use to describe the spiritual life, and indeed it is an image that is frequently used in the wider religious literature, is that of climbing a mountain. If you plan to climb a mountain, you first of all go out and take a look. You examine your options and see which routes you can take. You say, "Okay, we could go up this way. We could start here and we could go up that ridge, or we could go up the other side", and so on. There are many different ways up the mountain. There's no point in going two or three hundred meters up one track and then saying, "Oh, that was pretty good but I'll go back down now and try another route." You'll never get to the top of the mountain that way. The only way to get to the top of the mountain is to step onto one track and stay on it until you reach the top. Once you're at the top, it doesn't matter which track you came up, you are at the summit, you've reached the end of the journey. So yes, to answer your question, that is the whole point. That is the ultimate point of the spiritual life, that we should travel towards the center, the Absolute. You can, of course, describe that in all manner of different ways. You can call it discovering your true self, returning to your true being, becoming enlightened, receiving deliverance or salvation, or what have you. There's a vast range of different terminology we can use, but, to describe it in imagery, it is always a journey towards the center — or perhaps better, a *return* to the center.

What is everything in the modern world trying to persuade us to do? To go the other way. To make use of the diagram once more, if the religions are instructing us to look inward to the center — to the truth, the Absolute, the real — almost everything in the modern world is telling us to run the other way. They even go so far as to tell adherents of religions that they are in a box, a prison. They say, surely you don't want to be in there. It's repressive, authoritarian, patriarchal, superstitious, out-moded, oppressive. Get out of there and do your own thing! In effect, they are telling us to jump out of the outer ring, the exoteric tradition, into empty space!

What is in the empty space? All of the traits I mentioned earlier: confusion, ignorance, self-deception, hypocrisy, nihilism, chaos, dispersal, despair, and suicide, both literal and metaphoric. The modern world encourages people to attach themselves to all sorts of ephemeral false idols, to materialism — more TVs, more cars, more holidays, more superannuation, more power, more status, more sensual gratification, this thing, that thing and the other thing! As Buddhists, you know very well what all this amounts to. Attachment to such things, while not necessarily bad in themselves, doesn't bring us happiness or fulfillment; *they* are illusory "gods". They take us further away from the Center, further away from true fulfillment.

To return to your question, the answer, as I said, is yes. That is exactly what the traditionalists say: commit yourself to one tradition and practice its forms. Adopt what has been sanctioned and passed down by tradition and take that seriously. Don't imagine that you're above it. Don't imagine that it can be dispensed with. Don't sneer at the past. Don't take a condescending attitude. Regarding the past we should be doing precisely the opposite. And again, this is completely counter to the modern mentality in which everything new, young, and innovative is prized over the past. The past is viewed as a museum heap of debris, mere relics, because we have moved on now, we have "progressed". As I said before, as Buddhists, you should find the idea that the Buddha's teachings could be improved upon simply absurd. Nevertheless, there are plenty of Buddhists who are seduced by this sort of thinking. They say, let's take the findings of Buddha's teachings and beef them up a bit with the findings of modern science. Let's reconcile these two and we will be even better off. No, this won't work. It absolutely won't work. It is asking for trouble.

What we need is a framework which will allow us to situate the findings of science in their proper place. I am not saying that science has nothing to offer, that we can't learn something we didn't know before, that there's nothing to be gained from scientific discovery. But, generally speaking, the traditionalists take the view, and I'm certainly with them on this, that we know more and more about less and less. We know more and more about the material world: scientists can tell us everything about the reproductive system of insects, bacteria and so on, we can talk about gravity on Mars and outer space, or the mysteries of sub-atomic physics, but what does it all amount to? It amounts to a whole lot of data about the material world. And what has happened in the process? We have forgotten who we are, for we know less and less about ourselves, less and less about what it means to be a human. It is as if the more material knowledge we accumulate, the more our spiritual knowledge declines.

Let me give you an example. Let's say we have an Indigenous Australian woman out in the desert 300 years ago. Would she know anything about the theory of relativity? Absolutely nothing. Could she tell you how far Mars is from the next planet? No. She wouldn't know anything about computers, mobile phones, the internet, and so on. Imagine that next to her is a modern-day Professor of Nuclear Physics from the university. He has a string of degrees. He's read many tomes, he's written books, he can describe to you the theory of relativity, he knows how to get to the moon. He's got all the scientific information at his fingertips. Now, which one of these two people is wiser? I say the Aboriginal woman is wiser, because she knows something important. She knows something profound. She knows something worth knowing: she knows what it is to be a human being living in a sacred world. The professor doesn't know that. He might be the most educated man you can find, in modern terms, but he doesn't know that. And everything he knows is worth nothing compared to what she knows.

QUESTION: You seem to have quite a black and white approach to modernity. However, you mentioned that one of the reasons Buddhism could be spread in Tibet was that the Bön tradition there had become a bit dilapidated. Similarly, it seems to me that the traditions in the Western world were in a similarly dilapidated state and that is why modernity could come in and highlight all that was wrong with traditions and so challenge the traditions towards a deeper teaching argument. Because, as you said, in all traditions there are different levels of doctrine and method, and the way I see modernity is that it challenged the exoteric teachings towards a deeper teaching argument, which in turn made the traditions more available to ordinary people. In that sense, I think there's good news in modernity. It has shaken the traditions up a little bit, even if some of the traditions, such as the Christian tradition, still haven't responded in a deeper way.

HARRY OLDMEADOW: I can agree with you to this extent: there are undoubtedly, as I said before, certain compensations that modernity offers. Certain good things prevail in the modern world that didn't previously obtain. For example, the accessibility of Eastern teachings to people all around the world. These days, if someone is seriously interested in Eastern teachings, they can walk out of their front door, go down to their local bookshop or online, and buy a copy of the *Bhagavad Gita*, for instance, just like that. The world's spiritual riches are at our fingertips, accessible to all of us in a way that has never been so before. This is certainly a very good thing, a wonderful thing, but still, it is only a compensation.

When we look at the world as a whole and take everything into account, we do not say everything about tradition is good, nor do we say that everything about modernity is bad. We weigh up the good and the bad and when we then look at modernity as a whole, we find that in tradition there is a greater good and a lesser evil, whereas in modernity there is a lesser good and a greater evil. It is ridiculous to prefer a lesser good to a greater good. Therefore, insofar as we have to make a choice — and again, we don't necessarily have to think about it in terms of making a choice, but if we do — we must make a choice in favor of tradition, because that is where the greater good lies.

Let us take the case of Buddhism. Simply speaking, what does tradition offer us? Tradition offers us the teachings of the Buddha. It offers us the Sutras. It offers us all of the institutions which have evolved over hundreds of years, the sacred arts, the architecture, the practices, the meditations, the pilgrimages, the devotions, the whole kit and caboodle. On the other hand, what does modernity offer us? It offers us a more pluralistic world, a more open world in which certain things are more accessible, as you rightly say. Perhaps it offers us some modes of understanding, which weren't previously available, by way of modern science. That said, I myself take the view — and I admit that it's a minority view — that modern science is essentially a negation and essentially destructive. It purports to be is a value-free objective enquiry into the nature of the world so that we can understand how things really stand, but I don't think that's what modern science is at all.

Modern science is a worldview, an ideology, and far from being value-free, it is absolutely value-laden. And what is its basic function? Its basic function is to destroy traditional understandings because it cannot accommodate them, so it rubbishes them instead. It ignores them. It condescends to them. I don't mean any offence to individual scientists; I'm talking rather about principles and effects, about the general story of modern science. It is an extraordinarily arrogant collection of attitudes and views and mindsets which says everything people believed in the past all over the world in all cultures, without exception, was wrong. The only people who understand how things really are is we scientists, a very small group of people who have been present for a very short period of time, the last few hundred years, and in a particular culture, that of Western Europe and its extensions elsewhere. Everybody else is completely mistaken about things.

Q: Another issue is the religion of scientists. If a scientist is leaning towards the exoteric side, they will argue as you just explained. However, if you get a true scientist who is a truly spiritual person, although admittedly there are very few of them, they will be right in the center looking into the heart, beyond form, whether they are looking through a microscope or not.

HO: I have no problem with science in principle, but I would say this, I'll resort to an image the Sufis use, they say that modern science is like looking under Mother Nature's skirt. What do they mean? Modern science, in general, presumes that it can do anything. It believes that there is nothing that it cannot do, nothing that it cannot investigate and dissect, whether it be genetic engineering, cloning or whatever. Now that, I think, is the real danger. In this sense, what I'm really talking about is not science as such but *scientism* as an ideology, a set of values, attitudes, and beliefs. The idea that science doesn't have beliefs, that it doesn't rest on faith, that it doesn't rest on values, is fanciful. It does. For example, the faith of many modern scientists is, philosophically speaking, simply materialism. They believe that the material world exhausts reality, so if you want to understand reality you have to understand the material world. To go back to what you were saying before, while I appreciate your point and I partially agree with you, I nevertheless think that there is something very dangerous about looking through the microscope.

Q: Isn't that why we do meditation?

HO: Yes, but only metaphorically. In terms of meditation, what do we have on the side of tradition? In the case of Buddhism, we have two and a half thousand years of experience, we have two and a half thousand years of monks and nuns and sages and recluses, and even just ordinary householders, meditating, contemplating the nature of mind, the nature of consciousness. We have the most elaborate and sophisticated texts that you could imagine on this subject.

What have we on the side of modernity? We've got Freud, Jung, and some other thinkers, all these characters suddenly coming into the picture, as if this two and a half thousand years of experience counts for nothing, as if suddenly Dr. Freud discovered something that no one ever knew before. The idea is manifestly absurd. If we weren't seduced by this kind of evolutionist, progressivist notion that somehow we are coming to know more and more, somehow things are getting better, somehow we're gaining control of things, somehow science is giving us the answers, we would see that this is ludicrous. I'm not saying that what Freud said is wrong. I'm not saying that Freud didn't have some insights. He was a remarkable man, no question, and a very clever man, and he did have certain insights. However, to imagine that an entirely new way of understanding human behavior and experience, quite at odds with two and a half thousand years of meditational experience, could just appear and that we can now dispense with the great masters, such as Tsongkhapa and all the rest, because now we really know how it is, because modern science has told us so, that will not do. It will most certainly not do!

Moreover, many of the things that modern science tells us are not actually so. On the other hand, many of the things that people in the past told us, although materially inadequate — that is, not in conformity with the brute facts — are true at a much deeper level than anything science can tell us. The history books tell us that Copernicus and Galileo discovered that the earth is not the center of the solar system. Well, again, to imagine that nobody before Copernicus and Galileo had ever worked out that the earth wasn't the physical center of the solar system is quite simply wrong: the Egyptians knew it, the Greeks knew it, the Indians knew it. However, they also knew that a geocentric symbolism, whatever its material inaccuracies, was far preferable, far richer, far deeper, far truer in many other ways than what Galileo and Copernicus' discoveries promised to lead to, if pushed to their logical extreme, which they were. What did they lead to? They led to the idea that we live in a chaotic universe, a universe that is empty space with bits of debris floating around in it, and that earth is just one tiny speck of this debris and on this speck of debris, in this meaningless, chaotic universe, live organisms, you and me, who emerged out of some sort of primeval slime, and through mutation and the struggle for survival and natural selection, came to be what we now are. Well, for goodness sake, are you going to buy it? I'm not. I am not going to buy it. That is not who I am, it is not who you are, and you should know that perfectly well. If you are serious Buddhists and have studied your tradition and know what you're talking about, you will know that this is not who we are. We are not simply biological organisms!

QUESTION: When you talk about this inner circle on the diagram, which from my understanding is where a lot of indigenous societies are, it seems to me that as you move towards the Absolute you leave a lot of the shackles of the different religions behind. This is because you come to sense the living God within you and within every other human being and every other living thing, and so you actually don't need to go via someone or something else in order to get to God, because he's right there. As Krishnamurti said, you don't need a religion, you just need to talk to God.

HARRY OLDMEADOW: I have many problems with Krishnamurti, I must say. Nevertheless, Schuon would say, to use the Buddhist example, if you have attained the state of Buddhahood then you can dispense with the forms. However, until you have attained that state, you can't, which is to say that as long as we are still, to our varying degrees, living in a state of ignorance and confusion and alienation, we need the religious forms. That's the short answer.

Q: What is the status of the Buddha?

HO: That's another very big question. If we really go into it, we could be here for a very long time, so I'll just give a very brief explanation. There are those in the Theravadin tradition of Buddhism in particular who say that the Buddha was an ordinary human being who happened to get his act together. He was just like you and me, and he tried this, he tried that, he went into the forest, he practiced asceticism, he studied, and eventually he decided that the only way to do it was to sit down under the Bodhi tree and meditate until he attained final insight. This way of understanding the Buddha, in my opinion and also from a perennialist point of view, is an example of what the Buddhists call *upāya* — skillful or expedient means. It's a way of thinking about things which has a certain utility, but which is limited and which in the end turns out to be quite inadequate. The Mahayana tradition takes a much fuller view of the Buddha, I think, through the doctrine of the three *kayas*, the three bodies of the Buddha. Essentially, what the Mahayana teachings say, according to my understanding, is that the Buddha was an avatar. So, from this point of view, the Buddha is a cosmic savior. He was not an ordinary mortal.

Buddhism did not replace Hinduism; that was not its purpose. If that had been its providential role, Hinduism would have disappeared, in the same way that Roman paganism more or less disappeared through the advent of Christianity. However, Hinduism did not disappear and will not disappear because it is an integral tradition. Buddhism's relationship to Hinduism is very much like the relationship of Christianity and Islam to Judaism, which is to say, Buddhism came from the same soil, grew from the same seed, so to speak, and is a branch of the same tree. This being so, there is no fundamental rupture between Hinduism and Buddhism.

Someone might say, but of course there's a rupture, the two traditions are completely different: in Buddhism we don't have caste, we don't believe in Brahman, and so on and so forth. Nevertheless, it seems to me that the more you look at it, the more you discover that Hinduism and Buddhism are just two sides of the same coin, and that the Buddhist teachings about *shūnyatā* and the lack of self (the doctrine of *Anattā*) are just the negative version of what Hinduism teaches about Atman and Brahman. So, it is not and never was a question of Buddhism replacing Hinduism. Now, that's not to say that there weren't certain abuses and corruptions in Hinduism. That is no doubt one of the reasons that Buddhism appeared. But in any case, Buddhism, as well as being a branch from the same tree, offers everything needful, as all integral traditions do. There is no reason at all for any Buddhist to go outside the Buddhist tradition; there is nothing missing there.

This is another idea that the traditionalists emphasize, the idea that each tradition contains within itself all spiritual possibilities. In Buddhism, for example, there are the Pure Land schools, which are essentially forms of theistic Buddhism. On the face of it, you might think that this is impossible. How can you have a theistic Buddhist when Buddhism itself seems to be based on a non-theistic platform? And yet, in Japan, China, and other parts of the Far East we find the flourishing of Pure Land schools such as Jodo and Shin, which are theistic forms of Buddhism. This is because all spiritual possibilities must be represented within each tradition. It is quite silly to have arguments about which of the Buddhist schools is the most genuinely Buddhist. To argue about whether the Buddhism of Sri Lanka is more genuinely Buddhist than the Buddhism of Tibet, or Zen, or Jodo — these are futile arguments. They're not worth having.

QUESTION: I would say that my religion, if I can call it that, is democracy and freedom, and I feel incredibly fortunate and proud and happy to have lived in an era during which human rights are respected, in which I am free to express myself, to protest, where there is a free exchange of information and so on. It is, I think, not accidental that Buddhism is blossoming in the West. I believe this is largely thanks to the very freedom that we celebrate here, and this freedom has only come about in the last one hundred years. The fact that we have access to beautiful traditions such as Buddhism, that we can try to find some meaning there, is thanks to the fact that we are living in a new age, a new kind of era which lacks traditional forms, where, as someone previously mentioned, it's between us and God. What are your thoughts on this? Furthermore, today is September 11th and I wonder what you have to say about the apparent clash of cultures and civilizations, such that religion is persecuting the free world? Islam is coming after us, not the other way around.

HARRY OLDMEADOW: I'll address both questions at the same time, because they're related in some ways. The clash of religions in the modern world is lamentable, and very destructive, and the appearance of militant fundamentalism, not just in Islam but in several different religious traditions, is appalling and entirely regrettable and is leading to awful things around the world. On this I think we all agree.

Let us first look at Islamic fundamentalism. One way of understanding it is as a mistaken response to modernity. When I say mistaken I mean that its wellsprings, its motivating force is good, but it has taken a wrong turning somewhere and is traveling in the wrong direction altogether. What is the motivating force? The motivating force of this fundamentalism is a repudiation of modernity and an attempt to reaffirm tradition. Now, on the basis of everything I've said, I must be in favor of that. But of course, I'm not in favor of rampant fundamentalism and terrorism and everything else that goes with it.

On the other hand, what have we got in the modern world? You're saying that we've got freedom, respect for human rights and so on, and that these things didn't always obtain in the past, and that we should be grateful we have these things because they've created a world in which, for example, it's possible for us to know something about Buddhism and other traditions.

In the traditional world, let's say five or six hundred years ago, we find more or less homogeneous civilizations in all corners of the world, which is to say civilizations which are all of a piece, which hang together and have a certain coherence and unity. With modernity, this coherence and unity starts breaking down, because what happens is that, through the clash of cultures, imperialism, global communication and other factors, these various cultures start colliding with one another. Consequently, all sorts of antagonisms develop. In addition of course, there are sordid motivations by way of economic gain and political control, such as imperialism.

As we move closer and closer to the present, we arrive in a very pluralistic, very heterogeneous world, such as we now have in Australia where you find people from all over the world with all sorts of different beliefs. You might say, well, isn't it a good thing that we have freedom and that we respect human rights and that everyone can say what they think and so on? Yes, it is a very good thing. But you see, again, it is a compensation. What is better? The traditional world, such as Tibet five hundred years ago, in which cultures are more or less isolated, in which the ideas of tolerance, freedom, human rights are not really relevant, or what we've got now, a world where we have freedom, where we have an apparent respect for human rights, where we value dialogue and the like, but where the vast majority of the population has no spiritual life at all, where the overwhelming majority of the population has been completely seduced by the enticements of modernity?

You can't separate these things. You can't say, well, this and that in modernity is good and separate it from other parts of the picture. There are indeed many things that are good about modernity, but there are more things that are bad. You have to look at the total picture. I'm in favor of human rights and freedom, of course I am, but these are not absolute values. At least I don't think that they are absolute values. I don't think that they are sufficient to provide the basis for a civilization, just as they are not sufficient to provide the basis for a fulfilling and satisfying life for an individual. There has to be something more than that, and what I'm saying is that that something more will not and cannot be produced by modernity. You can be absolutely assured that it will not be produced by modernity. Many good things might be generated by modernity, but that's not one of them.

In other words, the only place you will find a doctrine and a method that is fully adequate is in tradition. Whether it be Buddhism, Christianity, or another tradition, it doesn't matter, but tradition is where you will find it. This is an "extreme" view, I know, and often people get upset and angry when I talk about this, but you're asking me so I'm telling you. From my point of view, you're not going to find an adequate doctrine and method through modern science or through modern psychology, and certainly the last place you're going to find it is in modern philosophy; only in tradition.

If ever there was a discipline and an enterprise which was devoted to the destruction of wisdom, the negation of wisdom, it is modern philosophy! As I said earlier, modern science is essentially negative, and philosophy is an accomplice of modern science. In fact, it is even worse. What does "philosophy" actually mean? It means the love of wisdom, the pursuit of wisdom in a practical sense. Why do we seek wisdom? So that we can live it, so that we can live a good fulfilling life! I've been to many Philosophy Departments around the world and I can assure you that the last thing academic philosophers (the vast majority at least) are interested in is the notion of wisdom and living a good life. That's not their aim at all. Rather their study of philosophy is an incredibly sterile kind of language game, an arena in which clever people develop ever more elaborate and ever more foolish theories. Postmodernist philosophy is there to prove it. That's what modern philosophy is all about. It's shocking, scandalous, the impoverishment of philosophy in modern times.

I'd say the same about a lot of psychology. Many people go to university to study psychology, thinking that they are going to learn about human consciousness, about human experience. Instead, they find out about the hardware in the brain, about rats, statistics, graphs, pie charts, and numbers. Precious little of it has much to do with human experience. Of course, it does vary. What I'm saying here is a reckless generalization, but certainly if you go to the Department of Psychology in most universities and talk to them about wisdom you do so at your peril: they'll look at you as if you're mad. They will tell you that they're only interested in what can be quantified, in what can be put on a chart, in what can be objectively established. So they'll wire you up to a computer, put wires in your ears, do this and that, because it's quantifiable, controllable data. It makes them feel powerful, it makes them feel like they have a handle on things. You cannot get a handle on the things that really matter through data. No way. That is the limitation of modern science, useful as it may be in its own domain.

QUESTION: I wonder if a woman could be speaking as you are, advocating tradition as you are, since women have been one of the main beneficiaries of the modern era?

HARRY OLDMEADOW: This is hazardous and difficult territory through which I must tread very carefully. There is no question that, in general, the traditions are patriarchal, that they are hierarchical, that they are authoritarian. Indeed, one of the issues which has arisen for Buddhism, in particular in its move to the West, is how to transplant a tradition which has been patriarchal, hierarchical, and authoritarian into a culture which is egalitarian, democratic, affirms the equality of sexes, and is committed to the liberation of women and men from sexual stereotypes, and so on and so forth.

As far as the question of democracy and hierarchy are concerned, I personally have no problems at all with the traditional view. I personally do not think that democratization is the way to go for Buddhist organizations. I think that, in the spiritual life, we have to recognize that there is a natural hierarchy, that we are not all starting at the same point. To believe that we are all at the same starting point is just sentimentality. We have to recognize that there are people who are more advanced than we are. You might point out that sometimes the hierarchy or leadership in institutions gets it wrong. Sometimes the person in charge is not the person who should be in charge, and so there are cases of abuse of power, of corruption. Sometimes bad things do happen. I don't deny any of that. I'm just talking about the principle. So, as far as the political principle is concerned, I myself have no problem with authoritarianism or hierarchy. Of course, the problem, in our sort of situation, is to make sure that the person who is in authority is the person who is most qualified to be in authority. In the traditional world, there are all sorts of safeguards, but in a modern environment it's a lot more difficult.

The question about gender is much more tricky. When I talk about this people often get upset. They think, who are you to talk about this issue? So, if you get upset by what I say, I'll understand, but I'm going to say it anyway. I have personally been very sympathetic to feminism, call it what you will, for more than 30 years. I hope my ideological credentials are in order. I am entirely sympathetic to the impulse of women to throw off patriarchal and other restrictions. But, how to feminize tradition, so to speak, how to find a balance between that and what has been sanctioned by tradition over all of these years is very difficult. It is very difficult.

I think it's clear that there are certain things we can do which are not destructive and which can be creative. We can certainly look to the traditions with different eyes, so to speak.

We can recuperate parts of the tradition which have been lost or which have been obscured or neglected because of patriarchy. In other words, we can rediscover the feminine in the tradition, whether it be in the form of women saints, women sages, representations of the feminine in sacred art and so on. We can bring these aspects to the forefront. We can bring these into the foreground and we can prize them and value them. There is no problem with this. However, whether this goes far enough or whether something more radical is required, it's very difficult to say. Should we have a female Dalai Lama, for example? Perhaps. I don't know.

Q: Many of the indigenous societies were matriarchal societies, and they haven't got the trappings of religion. What thoughts do you have on that?

HO: I must say that I'm a little skeptical about claims made about indigenous cultures and primal cultures being matriarchal. I think there has been an ideologically-motivated push in that direction amongst certain writers and scholars. I'm not saying that they are entirely wrong, but I think the picture is more complicated and ambiguous than they make out. Say we threw ourselves back 500 or 1000 years into Indigenous Australian society, before they had had any contact with the outside world. I would be surprised if the culture wasn't still essentially patriarchal, even if certain matriarchal elements were present. However, this is a historical argument.

QUESTION: My first observation is that traditionalism tends to be a procrustean bed, which tries to fit disparate traditions together. Guénon, to begin with, distinguished between what he called metaphysical tradition – and his paradigm was the Vedanta, which has notions of an Absolute – and religious tradition, so that, in particular, the monotheisms don't fit very well with Buddhism, which is a quite different tradition.

Also, I don't think that Buddhism fits very well into the paradigm for other sorts of reasons: one is that there's much more room in Buddhism for "I don't know", there's much more tolerance of uncertainty. You mentioned Chaos theory, and I think that Buddhism lives much better with uncertainty than other traditions. One of the problems that I have with the traditionalist viewpoint is that they tend to adopt a very combative view, as if they know all the answers. I suspect that this comes from the roots of traditionalism in the Gnostic movement of the 19th century which preceded it, Martinism, Theosophy and so forth. That's the first point I'd like to make.

The second point is Guénon's use of the Hindu system of cycles to represent time in *The Reign of Quantity and the Signs of the Times*. Really, if René were alive at this moment, he would say, I told you so, it's all happening faster and faster. The question is, what can we do in the modern world? Apart from practicing traditions and watering our own gardens, there's nothing we can do to stop the progress of quantification in the modern world. The traditionalists don't seem to give any scenario for what happens at the end of the cycle. Is it all going to go up in some kind of cataclysm? Some deluge? And are the spiritual elite, those who have the inside knowledge and the traditions, going to be there to act as the new leaders of society? That seems to be something which is hinted at, but it's not spelled out. All the writers, Nasr, Sherrard and so forth, have written books about the evils of the modern world. We know that all too well. But what is going to replace it?

HARRY OLDMEADOW: Although the discussion of the end of the world, the end of the cycle is interesting and although

I take it very seriously, I myself take the view that, on an individual level, it's best not to get too involved with all of that, because it can very easily lead to despair and negativity and a feeling of hopelessness. The situation is never hopeless. No matter what cyclic conditions obtain, no matter where we are in the cycle. As long as we're here, as long as the world is here, the possibility of liberation is here, the possibility of sanctification is here. So, whatever the situation, whatever the conditions obtaining in the outer world, our task remains the same. Our task is to continue on the spiritual journey. If we are Buddhists we have certain things that we must be doing as we go along. We must fill our lives with wisdom, with compassion, with compassionate activity. This is not conditional. The Buddha didn't say, well, you can do this in certain circumstances, but not in other circumstances. This is what you do, regardless of the situation. This being so, if you're committed to a particular religious path, whether Buddhist or something else, it is very clear what you need to do.

Of course, that doesn't mean that it's easy, because most of us don't actually want to do it. We say we want to do it, but we don't really, because we're lazy, because we're ruled by our passions, because we're attached to so many things, seduced by distractions of one sort and another. We have an endless litany of excuses why we shouldn't do something at this particular moment. Nevertheless, what we should do and what we need to do is all there. It's all spelled out quite clearly. So that is what we need to be doing, whatever the external conditions are.

If we do that, we cannot help but benefit the surrounding world. The person sitting in a cave in the Himalayas meditating on the teachings of the Buddha is doing the rest of us an incalculable benefit, perhaps far more benefit than the person building hospitals and roads and doing good works all about the place. This is another kind of prejudice, a superstition of the modern world, that we all should be rushing about doing good works. Good works have their place, they're a very beneficial thing. But anybody, anybody who is on the spiritual path, cannot but generate good for the surrounding environment, so that's all we need to worry about. That's what we need to be doing.

We need to be traveling that path. We need to be doing whatever is required by the traditional forms. And if we're doing that, we're doing everything that is needful, and we needn't worry ourselves about the end of the world. If the end of the world is coming, it's coming. It doesn't mean that we should throw the towel in or put ourselves in a hole in the ground. It doesn't mean that we should eat, drink, and be merry because tomorrow everything's going to close down. You just go on doing what you're supposed to be doing, regardless. That's the right thing to be doing.

BUDDHISM AND THE SPIRITUAL ENCOUNTER OF EAST AND WEST

Why is it that the fate of Tibet has found such a deep echo in the world? There can only be one answer: Tibet has become the symbol of all that present-day humanity is longing for, either because it has been lost or not yet realized or because it is in danger of disappearing from human sight: the stability of a tradition, which has its roots not only in a historical or cultural past, but within the innermost being of man, in whose depth the past is enshrined as an ever-present source of inspiration.

– Lama Anagarika Govinda

P REVIOUSLY I spoke about the traditionalist understanding of religion and about modernity in general. Tonight I would like to discuss two themes: first of all, the challenges of modernity to religion in general and to Buddhism in particular, and secondly, the particular problems that face Eastern religious traditions, such as Buddhism, when they are transplanted to the West.

THE CHALLENGES OF MODERNITY TO RELIGION

To begin with, a brief overview of the last few hundred years to establish what the characteristics of modernity actually are. I will then talk about why I think modernity poses serious problems for all religious traditions.

The Tyranny of Modern Science

The story we are told in the history books is that, once upon a time, people lived in the Dark Ages and their understanding of things was very limited. In their ignorance, they were prey to all sorts of religious superstitions. Then, with the Renaissance and the Scientific Revolution that followed, suddenly many things were illuminated and we came to understand the world and our place in it much better. We are told that science revealed to us all manner of things so that we are now in a position to understand our world and ourselves much better.

What was this science all about? Figures of the 17th century, such as Galileo, Copernicus, and Newton, inaugurated a trend that has been continuing ever since. It was a change that gradually formed the modern mentality, so that science is now the basis upon which most people understand the world; most people now believe that science provides us with the most comprehensive and reliable account of reality. Modern science as we know it is very different from traditional science, such as we find in Asia as well as in the West in earlier times. Modern science is essentially materialistic, which is to say that it deals with material reality. It is a way of getting a hold on material phenomena. That, in itself, is fine. The problem is that the *ideology* or philosophy of modern science has persuaded us that reality is material. This is a very big jump. Modern science is quite unable to deal with anything of an immaterial order, of a spiritual order, and so it generally takes one of three tacks: it ignores all non-material dimensions of reality; or it treats non-material realities as mere epiphenomena which issue from matter; or, worst of all, it denies that they exist.

To summarise, science and its accompanying philosophy are materialistic (in the philosophical sense). Secondly, science is rationalistic, which is to say that it has elevated and exalted reason as the instrument of knowledge. (There is a philosophical contradiction between materialism and rationalism but this is a subject we can't explore here). It regards reason as the supreme faculty of the human mind. Thirdly, modern science is empirical. It bases its knowledge, if that is what it is, on the observation of material phenomena that are accessible to the senses: material phenomena that can be seen, heard, felt, touched, that can be observed under a microscope, placed above a Bunsen burner, that can be wired, measured, and so on and so forth. It has developed the "scientific method" of hypothesis, observation, experimentation, and verification.

These scientific procedures for investigating the material world would, in normal circumstances, be more or less harmless and sometimes beneficial. The problem is that science has gone far beyond its level of competence and has become a worldview (i.e. *scientism*), a way of explaining reality, of explaining life and the human being. From my point of view, the explanation that science offers us is a very one-dimensional and impoverished explanation. Nevertheless, it has tremendous status in the modern world. If science says something is so, then most of us take it for granted that indeed it is so.

It's interesting that, when we look at the history of science, what we see happening over and over again is one scientific theory being replaced by another. At any given moment, people think that they've finally explained how things are. They say, "Well, we used to think such and such, but now we know that actually this is the case." And so the old theory, hypothesis, or paradigm is abandoned and replaced with a new one. This process has been going on for hundreds of years, and no doubt it will continue. The problem is that people take the philosophies and theories that are currently in vogue not to be provisional hypotheses, but to be fact. They forget that scientific theories, constructs, and paradigms *always* collapse. In the end, they always collapse and are replaced with something else.

For example, at present, the reigning orthodoxy in the biological sciences is evolutionism. More or less everyone, certainly amongst the educated segment of the population, takes it for granted that the theory of evolution is factual, that it is firmly based on empirical evidence and that it is incontrovertible. Anyone who contests it is regarded as a crank, a fundamentalist, an obscurantist. In other words, any intellectual or philosophical opposition to the theory of evolution is simply dismissed. Such objections have no credibility amongst the intelligentsia. Nevertheless, I am absolutely sure that in 50, 100, or 150 years from now, the theory of evolution will go the same way that all other scientific theories before it have gone, which is to say that it will be disposed of. It will be shown to be fallacious from all sorts of points of view, especially in its seminal conception of the transformation of species. Moreover, the theory of evolution is particularly damaging because it is allied with another one of the false idols of the modern world, another shibboleth, and that is the idea of progress. We cannot lay this entirely at the door of science; there are all manner of factors that have led to the creation of this pseudo-myth. Still, it is astonishing what a grip it has on the modern mind. One would have thought that the evidence to the contrary was so overwhelming that this idea of progress would have long since been abandoned. How it could possibly survive the 20th century is one of the great mysteries of modern times. I emphasise this theme of "progress" because I think it's very important in the context of the encounter of East and West and the situation facing Eastern religions in the West today, a subject to which we will turn presently.

To reiterate, we have a materialistic, rationalistic, empirical science that is informing and shaping the prevailing worldview. This science propounds several theories, such as evolutionism, as well as various kinds of psychological theories. These psychological theories don't have the same totalitarian influence that evolutionism does, but nevertheless they have sunk pretty deep into the modern mentality. Freud is regarded as the inaugurator of modern psychology, but subsequently we've seen all kinds of theories ramify in all directions. However, the basic idea common to them all is that human behaviour, human experience, human consciousness can be explained in purely psychological terms. Now, as you know, Buddhism is very interested in psychology, in consciousness, and it has developed an elaborate psychology of its own. This then would seem to be a contact point which is perhaps fertile ground for Western science and Eastern religion to meet. What I would suggest is that, although there may indeed be some possibilities here, the whole thing is fraught with danger, the reasons for which I will explain in a moment.

Philosophical Relativism: "There is No Such Thing as Truth"

Another development in the modern world that poses a challenge for a religious understanding of things is philosophical relativism. Nietzsche is the main culprit here, but he is not the only one. Nietzsche pronounced that there are no absolute truths, that nothing whatsoever is absolutely true. Things are only relatively true, he claimed: true from a certain point of view, in a certain context, for certain people, but never absolutely true. He talked about "perspectivism", asserting that there is no Archimedean point from which we can look, from which we can have an objective view; rather, we are all enmeshed in the situation and so can only understand things partially, from a particular point of view. There are no unchanging truths according to Nietzsche. This is, of course, a theme that has been taken up by the postmodernist theorists in a very extravagant way, so much so that it has become very corrosive. The very idea of truth is now, it seems, hopelessly compromised. To talk in intellectual, philosophical, or academic circles as if there is such a thing as truth is to immediately invite the accusation that one is "naïve", or "romantic" or "old-hat". The notion of objective truth is not to be taken seriously anymore. Who wants to be "old-hat"?

Nietzsche dismissed all previous philosophising, of the Western world at least, by asking, what is philosophy? His answer was that all works of philosophy – and here he is referring to Plato and all other philosophers ever since – are nothing but "involuntary memoirs". In other words, someone's philosophy tells us more about the individual than anything else; philosophy is a kind of camouflaged autobiography that tells us something about the person who constructed the philosophy and articulated it, but does not tell us anything about reality. It does not enshrine a non-subjective truth in any kind of way. In this respect, he anticipates Freud, because one of Freud's central themes is that we are not the rational creatures we think we are, but rather are governed by all sorts of impulses, forces, and complexes of which we are quite unaware. These outlooks are highly problematic as far as a religious understanding of things is concerned.

"Naturalised" Prejudices: Democracy and More

In the modern world, there are many ideas that have become naturalised, so to speak. What do I mean by "naturalised"? I mean that we have been indoctrinated into various ideas to such a degree that we no longer question them. We take them to be self-evident truths, but I think that, if we take a long view and examine these things carefully, they are not self-evident truths at all. Rather, they are fashionable prejudices, fashionable tastes, biases, inclinations, dispositions. So ingrained are they that they often become invisible, so to speak

The idea of democracy is one example. In the modern Western world, amongst the educated classes at least, it's taken for granted that democracy is the best system, the best of all possible worlds. Other possibilities are very rarely discussed. "Everybody knows" that democracy, together with egalitarianism, equal opportunity and the like are self-evidently true and that there could not possibly be any serious debate about it. Anyone who does want to debate these issues is regarded as a fascist or authoritarian or some kind of relic from the out-dated past, an intellectual dinosaur.

I myself am rather inclined to Plato's view of democracy. Plato took the view, two and a half thousand years ago, that, just as there are four great cycles in human and cosmic time, so too there are four systems in the social and political order that move through a descending cycle. It is interesting that the four cycles and the four systems of government correspond very closely to the four castes in the traditional Hindu social order. In Plato's view, the best of all possible forms of government is that of the Philosopher King, which in the Indian context would be the rule of the Brahmins, followed by the rule of the Warriors, followed by the rule of the Merchants, followed by the rule of the People. The problem with the rule of the people (democracy), according to Plato, is that it leads to tyranny. Again, one would have thought, given the history of the 20th century, that this idea might have presented itself to the modern mentality, but so tenacious is the grip of the democratic ideal that the more sinister and darker sides of democracy or popular rule are very rarely canvassed in the modern world.

The Temptation of Compromising with Modernity

I mention these ideas because they have some bearing on my next topic: the situation of Eastern religious traditions trying to find a place and make their way in the modern Western world.

All of the issues I have mentioned pose very serious challenges to traditions such as Tibetan Buddhism. Given the pervasive power of the modern mentality that I've been describing, it is easy to see how, when a tradition moves from the East into this kind of climate, it must be extremely tempting to accommodate this kind of mentality, if not surrender to it altogether.

My view, elaborated in last week's talk, is that it is not the place of a religious tradition to compromise with, make accommodations for, or change its fundamental nature in the face of these forces of modernity. Rather, it should be holding its ground, holding fast to what has served it so well for thousands of years, namely its traditional forms, practices, doctrines, art and so on. Of course, I realize that things aren't that simple. You cannot just plop an Eastern tradition into a modern, pluralistic, liberal, secular, urbanised, capitalistic, consumerist society and say, "Well, here we are, come and get it". Of course you have to in some way take account of the environment in which you find yourself. But, from my point of view – and I know that many people disagree with me – the great danger for traditions such as Tibetan Buddhism in the modern West is that they go too far in making these accommodations. What will happen, if that is the case? Tibetan Buddhism, or Buddhism in general, will gradually, over a period of time, become diluted. It will be compromised, it will be bastardised, and as a result it will turn into just another one of an endless variety of pseudo-spiritual philosophies and practices. If it wants to retain its vitality, its potency, its universal message, if it wants to fulfil its providential function in the modern world, then I think it must hold fast to tradition insofar as that is possible. Now, let me mention several areas that I think are problematic for traditions such as Tibetan Buddhism in the modern West.

Problems Facing Eastern Religious Traditions in the Modern West

Transmission

First of all, there is the problem of transmission. In places like traditional Tibet, there was a carefully controlled transmission of spiritual authority through the lineages. Generally speaking, this took place within a monastic framework, and of course that system was not foolproof. I don't want to present past structures as some kind of perfect, utopian model. They were not perfect. No society, anywhere, at anytime, has ever been utopian or perfect. All societies without exception — for this is the nature of things, the nature of human beings, the nature of the social order — are a mixture of good and bad. They all have their strengths and weaknesses. They are all liable to corruptions, to decadence, to abuses, to injustice, to oppression, and so on, as we know. The question is, when we take the whole picture into account and look at all the different aspects of society together, from a religious or spiritual point of view, particularly in this context, we have to ask ourselves the question, where lies the greater good and the lesser evil?

People are usually very quick to bring up the shortcomings of traditional societies, be it in Tibet, medieval Europe, ancient India or wherever. They will point to cases of abuse, oppression and the like, certain groups treated cruelly, slavery, persecutions, awful wars. Yes, these things happened, they did occur, and no one is condoning or justifying them. That is not the issue. The question is not whether there were abuses in traditional societies; of course there were. The question is, if we take a general overview and think in very large terms, when we look at the abuses in traditional societies and compare them with the abuses in our modern society, where do we find the greater abuses? In my mind, there is no question; it is in our modern society that we find the greater abuses. Likewise, where are to be found the greater goods? I myself do not doubt that they are to be found in traditional cultures.

In any case, to return to the issue of transmission. How is authority passed from one generation to the next? How is the integrity of the doctrine preserved through this transmission? We know how it was done in Tibet. They had a centuries-old system that, on the whole, worked very well. However, in our environment – secular, urban, liberal, pluralistic, heterogeneous and all the rest – it is very difficult to preserve the same institutional structures that ensured an uninterrupted transmission in the four great lineages of Tibetan Buddhism. Thus, the question of transmission is, I think, a challenging one for Tibetan Buddhism in the West.

Authority and Governance

Secondly, there is the related question of authority and governance. Again, we can contrast the situation in Tibet in former times with the current situation in the modern West. Does the authority of the teacher derive from initiation and transmission? Or does it derive from the approval and sanction of the community that the teacher is serving? Do we want, should we want, to retain the very finely calibrated hierarchies that we find in traditional monastic life? Or do we want a much more open, democratic kind of system where everybody has a say, where there is a voting system and the like?

Given what I said above about democracy, it's not surprising to find that most Western Buddhists are very much in favour of democratic models of governance. I'm reminded of the remark of Ananda Coomaraswamy on this subject. He said, "I don't want to be ruled by my equals. I want to be ruled by my betters". But the very idea that we might have betters is not an idea that's palatable to the modern mind. Still, I think it's one that people involved in such situations need to think about. Can matters concerning the spiritual life, doctrine, practice, and so on, be subjects for "consensus"? I myself do not think so. I think this flies in the face of the irrefutable fact that some people are much more advanced on the spiritual path than others. This should be recognised in structures of governance as well as in other matters.

The Teachings

The third question concerns the teachings. Is there a "pure" Buddhist teaching? This is a subject that has generated a lot of debate. Is there an essential, inviolate core of teaching, which always remains the same and should always remain the same? If there is, how can we distinguish it from cultural accretions and more or less accidental additions that they have accumulated in a particular culture over a period of time but which are not essential and which can be relinquished without diminishing the essential message? And who is to decide what is essential and what is not?

The Lay Environment

Another issue is the lay environment. We are dealing with a tradition that in Tibet was oriented around monasteries and monastic orders, but here in the West the situation is entirely different. Most of the people involved in Tibetan Buddhism in the West are not monks and nuns, but ordinary lay folk. What kind of implications does this have? This is another issue.

Charismatic Leadership

Fifth, charismatic leadership. This is a very serious problem and one that is particularly evident in North America at the moment. Many of the first generation of teachers who travelled from Tibet, India and other such places to North America established institutes, libraries, communities, monasteries, meditation centers and the like. Many of these teachers were charismatic, spellbinding personalities. I am referring to figures such as Chögyam Trungpa, Tarthang Tulku, Namkhai Norbu, and the Karmapa, amongst many others. Their appeal to contemporary Americans derived largely from their charismatic personalities. What happens then when they die? All sorts of problems arise in their absence. We are now in the next generation. Most of these first-wave leaders have died, leaving a vacuum in which problems of one sort or another have arisen.

Gender

A sixth issue concerns gender. This is obviously an important yet difficult one. There are all manner of debates taking place about the way that gender is understood and represented, the role of women within the traditional Buddhist forms, both in Tibet and outside, and so on. The arrival of Buddhism in the West has necessitated a re-examination of understandings of and attitudes towards gender. We know from research that the majority of

Buddhist practitioners in North America today are women, and the same is most likely true for Australia and other Western countries. This presents certain questions about the patriarchal structures which have obtained in the East.

Abuse

Then there is the volatile issue of abuse. I don't want to dwell on this, but it would be disingenuous to ignore it. The issue of teachers abusing their positions through their charisma, their office, their institutional position and so on is not something peculiar to Buddhism. We find it in varying forms in all sorts of religions and elsewhere. However, I must say that anyone who takes a dispassionate look at what has happened in North America, particularly over the last 30 or 40 years, will, to say the least, find grounds for some discomfort. We don't want to overdramatise this issue, but we cannot ignore three kinds of problems that have frequently reared their heads: sexual exploitation, the misuse of funds, and the pursuit of a lifestyle that appears to be at radical odds with what is being taught. These problems have manifested themselves in the behaviour of both Easterners — Indians, Tibetans, Japanese or whoever — and their Western followers, those who have been initiated and sanctioned as teachers and leaders. There have been some very bizarre and sordid episodes, so this is another problem.

The Relationship of Ethnic and Western Buddhists

Another issue in the West is the tension between ethnic and Western Buddhists. I'm not really familiar with the scene in Australia on this front, but I do know that in North America there are two kinds of Buddhist communities: the communities of Asian refugees and expatriates (Koreans, Japanese, Tibetans, Indians, and so on) and the communities of Western Buddhists. By and large, they keep separate and have very little to do with each other. They have their own institutions, their own practices, and their own teachers. This situation cannot go on indefinitely. I think that some sort of coming-together has to take place.

Applying the Teachings to Everyday Life

Then there are a range of issues for the ordinary lay practitioners, who are the vast majority in the West, regarding the relation of Dharma teachings to everyday life, to work and family life, and the like. Obviously these questions arise in the very different kind of social environment from the one that applied in traditional Tibet, India or elsewhere in the East.

Global Challenges

Leaving aside these particular problems, it seems to me that there are two more pervasive, global challenges that also need to be addressed. Firstly, the relationship of the different religions to one another. I touched on this last week. I believe that what is required is a recognition of diversity, a respect for other religions, and an understanding that the different traditions are all valid in their own way, but, at the same time, a philosophical platform for understanding how they converge and what they have in common. I think this is necessary in order, amongst other things, to provide a united front, if that's not too militant a metaphor, against the myriad anti-religious forces of the modern world. This is one big challenge.

The second is a political challenge. What are we to do about the state of the world that we are living in, this extraordinary mess? In this world we have created every conceivable kind of problem: the world is ravaged by war, by racism, by consumerism, by genocide, by the displacement of peoples, by the despoliation of the environment... the list is endless. So, what can a tradition like Tibetan Buddhism, perhaps in cooperative alliance with other religions, actually do about these problems? What is the best way of dealing with them? In this regard, I think that Tibetan Buddhism has an extraordinary amount to offer, and there are several reasons for that. Tibetan Buddhism has been much less torn by sectarian strife than most other religious traditions. It has generally adopted a much more hospitable, open, friendly, and accommodating attitude to other religions. So, in this light, I think it has a lot to teach some of the other traditions.

To return to my earlier point, most people in the modern world imagine that we will solve the problem with more of the same, which is to say, more science, more technology, more rationalism, more empiricism, etc. This is completely illogical. It is these things that have led us into this situation. What we now need are some alternatives. We need to be looking outside the box as they say. We need to be looking for a different kind of answer altogether. I do not say that Buddhism is the only place by any means. There are many places we might look, such as, for example, the indigenous traditions. The pre-modern West also has a lot to offer, but I think the Eastern traditions do too, and in some ways they might be the most accessible for many contemporary Westerners. This being so, the Eastern traditions might be their easiest route out of the worldview and mindset that we are locked into.

QUESTION: What do you mean by the "pre-modern West"?

HARRY OLDMEADOW: To cut a very long story short and to make it much simpler than it is, my view of things is that the West, or the European world, up until the end of the Middle Ages, was a traditional world. It had certain characteristics that all traditional cultures have, and my general view is that traditional societies are, on the whole, preferable. Despite their abuses, they are preferable to modern societies, which are essentially anti-traditional.

The reigning worldview in the modern Western world has come into being since the end of the Middle Ages. It really started with the Renaissance. Everything that's happened since – the Reformation, the Scientific Revolution, the Industrial Revolution, the Enlightenment, Darwinian science, Freudian psychology, the whole box and dice, right down to postmodernist theorizing – has created a worldview, an understanding, which is anti-traditional. The past is regarded in almost entirely negative terms. How do we think about the past? Often we think of people who didn't understand how things work, who were riddled with strange beliefs and funny customs. We might regard some of their practices as quaint and interesting, but we cannot take them seriously. This is the general modern view.

What I'm arguing is that the condition in which the world finds itself, fraught with problems, is simply a reflection of what is going on within us, collectively. To take one example, the fact that the external, material world is in such a mess, that we have created an environmental crisis, is a reflection of our collective consciousness. The environmental crisis is a visible outer symptom, a kind of mirror of our inner alienation, confusion, ignorance. We couldn't possibly desecrate and destroy the natural order unless we were ignorant and confused and alienated, not to mention a whole lot of other things — like extraordinarily arrogant.

So, how do we find our way out of this mess? The reply most people give is, more of the same, more science, more technology, more money. They believe that science will solve the problem. However, the fact is that the science has, in large measure, *created* the problem. We need to look outside that, outside this modern mindset, for an alternative way of understanding, a better way of understanding. For this, I suggest indigenous cultures, I suggest the traditions of the East, but I also suggest the pre-modern West, for there is a great deal of richness, profundity, and wisdom in the Western tradition if we go back far enough. There's no use looking in the last few hundred years. There you will just find various forms of ignorance. If, however, we go back to medieval Europe, or even further back, we will find a wisdom there which can give us a new angle on the contemporary situation. It could be Celtic mythology, or classical philosophy, or mystical Christianity. All of these traditions and cultures, along with Buddhism, Hinduism, Taoism, Confucianism, the American Indians and so on, have crucial things in common. The modern world has broken away from them and that is why it is in such a plight.

To give one very obvious example. In all traditional cultures, we find a sense of the sacred. We find the idea of a dimension of the world, of ourselves, of life, of reality, that is inviolate, that is an absolute good, and which we ought to revere, before which we ought to feel humbled, to which we ought to be receptive. Scientific materialism, the modern mentality, cannot cope with this. They say, "What is all this foolish talk about 'the 'sacred'? It's simply a psychological projection, or an infantile complex, or a search for security, or a symptom of childish naiveté when we know that there's really nothing there." With such "explanations", they reduce and dismiss the sense of the sacred which is intuitive in all peoples everywhere except in the modern West. A sense of the sacred is a birthright of humankind and we stifle it at our peril. As long as we go on doing that, we are exacerbating the problem, making it worse and worse. The more convinced we are that we are grown-up, that we've got our feet on the ground, that we understand what's what, and that anyone who thinks differently is childish – as long as we think this way, there's no turning back and the road to catastrophe stretches out before us as clear as day. Nothing can be surer than if we keep going the way we've been going for the last three or four hundred years. There's only one possible end to it all, and that is catastrophe. What form the catastrophe will take, I don't know. Will it be a global war? Will it be a nuclear holocaust? Will it be the destruction of the environment? Will it be genetic mutation? I don't know, but I do know that if we don't turn around, if we don't change direction, that's it, the show is over.

QUESTION: The Renaissance saw the arising of ethnocentrism, placing man at the center of the world rather than God. When you say "go back to sacredness", I like this idea. However, in the past sacredness was connected with something external, and so I wonder, what do you say to that? Can we bring some sense of sacredness into our lives and at the same time keep man in the center, rather than searching for a deity or external god?

HARRY OLDMEADOW: This is a very good question. There is no doubt that ethnocentrism was one of the main projects of the Renaissance: humanism, an anthropocentric kind of understanding that regards man as the measure of all things, thereby asserting the dignity of the human individual and so on. Now, to a certain extent, I have some time and respect for that. However, I think it's out of control and grown out of proportion.

It has become a kind of cult of individualism in the modern world, and this is a very dangerous thing.

Let us have a look at the difference between traditional Buddhist psychology and modern Western psychology. What is modern Western psychology, essentially? Well, we could give all manner of answers, but one answer is that it is about the rehabilitation and reinforcement of the ego. You might have a person with low self-esteem, or a particular pathology or trauma, perhaps a guilt complex for example. What we need to do, according to Western psychology, is fix them up, by whatever means, so that they feel good about themselves and so they are socially "functional". What does this amount to? It amounts to bolstering the ego, so that the person has a strong sense of self and can function in the so-called world. If a person is in a mess, that's a reasonable approach, no question. I have no argument with that. If a person is riddled with guilt, trauma, or neurosis, that is a way of repairing the situation. It is, however, a completely different approach to Buddhist psychology. The end goal in Buddhist psychology is precisely the opposite: the dismantlement of the ego. That is the ultimate end. It might take a very long time to get there, but that's where we're heading. That's what we're trying to do. We're trying to free ourselves from our attachment to the ego. Western psychology is part and parcel of the individualism of the modern mindset, the absolute value of individualism, the individual being the center of experience, the center of the world. With this view, we want to prop the individual up and hold the individual together at all costs. Maybe this is limited thinking, when we compare it with the Buddhist teaching, because what we really want in the end is to free ourselves from the tyranny of the ego and its desire, attachment, aversion, and so on.

To return to your question about the sense of the sacred. I think that the short answer to your question is no. Can we have a sense of the sacred located merely in the individual without reference to anything external by way of deities or the like? I know that many Buddhists won't agree with me on this particular issue, but my answer is no, you cannot. There has to be something beyond the individual. Even in Buddhism, with its focus on the individual and on direct experience, its empirical emphasis, what do we have to do to be serious Buddhist practitioners? We have to take refuge in the Buddha, the Dharma, and the Sangha. They are something external, from a certain point of view. Yet, as a Buddhist, one has to take refuge in the "Three Jewels" as absolute goods, in principle at least. Abuses can take place and so on, but in principle they are absolute goods. Moreover, Buddhism in Tibet, in actual practice, was devotional for the majority. The Tibetan Buddhist tradition, not to mention other branches of Buddhism, is full of deities and bodhisattvas and other revered beings. I think that the devotional impulse, like the sense of the sacred, is inherent in human beings; we have the natural impulse for reverence and for what the Hindus call *bhakti-yoga*. It is part of the human makeup. But where is this impulse directed in the modern world? In all sorts of ludicrous places, either onto the self and the pursuit of a completely self-centered, hedonistic lifestyle, or onto celebrities like Kylie Minogue, or football players, for example, who become mythologized and take on a surreal life of their own. The grotesqueries of the cult of Celebrity! Human nature longs for something sacred, is always searching for something sacred, something to which we can devote ourselves, something for which we can feel reverence. In the modern world, because religion is in such disarray, there are all sorts of pseudo-alternatives, and this doesn't make people happy, of course, just more confused and unhappy.

QUESTION: Can devotional impulses be positive and non-religious? HARRY OLDMEADOW: Yes, I'm sure this impulse sometimes gets channelled in directions that might be positive and beneficial, at least in the short-term, but I think that, in the end, you need an absolute good, whether it be found in nature, in tradition, in deities, in saints, in bodhisattvas, or elsewhere. So I think you do need something outside, so to speak. Buddhist philosophy would say that ultimately there is no "inside" and there is no "outside", so in the end the question itself doesn't matter, but most of us aren't yet at that level of understanding so we needn't presently concern ourselves with that question.

QUESTION: One of the other things about this focus on the ego is not facing anything. One of the things that I learnt when I was with the Shuar [the indigenous people of Ecuador and Peru] is that their philosophy is to face anything that comes to them. In our society, however, we turn away from things and hide with medication, for example, and the next thing we do is find someone to blame. We don't look at solving the problem. It's just, who can we blame? Our parents, the fact that I didn't have a teddy bear, the people next door didn't like me, and things like that.
HARRY OLDMEADOW: These tendencies are the legacy of a certain form of psychology that believes that people only behave in certain ways and only feel certain things because they've had certain experiences. Although it need not, this approach can easily discourage people from taking responsibility for themselves. Now, of course, this is not to deny that many people undergo terrible experiences that leave deep scars, and that we should

feel compassion and so on. Nevertheless, there is something unhealthy about the modern tendency to explain away and, in a sense, to accept or condone certain habits or behaviour on the grounds that a person suffered a traumatic childhood, that they had an abusive mother or father, or they lived in poverty, whatever the case may be.

Here again, I think that the essential Buddhist teachings have so much to offer, if only people would listen to them, if only people would hear them. The late Shunryu Suzuki, one of the first Zen teachers in North America, was once asked during a gathering if he could please sum up the message of Buddhism in one sentence. He thought about it for a moment, and then said, "Not always so" (i.e. everything changes). That was his answer: impermanence. By way of contrast, what do we have in the modern world? We have many people – including myself – rushing around in a frenzy attaching themselves to something that they think is going to give them happiness. Maybe it's status, maybe it's power, maybe it's wealth, maybe it's sensual gratification. Whatever it is, we pursue it thinking, "If only I can get this thing then everything will be hunky-dory. I will be happy". We don't have to study the Buddhist teachings for very long to know that this is not true. Everything will not be hunky-dory, because everything is impermanent, everything comes and goes, all material things that is, all things in the time-space world of relativities; all material, composite things come and go. The Buddha and his teaching do not come and go.

Take another example; think about contemporary, modern Western attitudes to death. We live in a death-denying society. People do not want to know about it. Any talk of death makes many people feel uncomfortable. They'd rather turn their backs and not think about it. Yet death is one of the central themes of Buddhist meditation: learning how to face and deal with death, to accept death as part of life. We modern, Western people, however, are running in the opposite direction. But, no matter how fast or how far we run, in the end death always catches up with us through the deaths of our loved ones and eventually of ourselves. Sadly, because of our anxieties and neuroses about death, we aren't able to deal with it. I'm speaking in reckless generalisations of course, but this is the case for a great many people. They are so much in denial of death that when someone close to them dies, they've no idea how to behave and find themselves unable to exercise compassion, support, warmth, and love. Such is the modern attitude to death – excessive fear and denial.

The most basic teachings of Buddhism, or indeed any other religious tradition, are tremendous antidotes to this modern madness. But of course, as long as people are convinced that society is "progressing", that science has the answers, that we live in the best of all possible worlds, that we know better than our ancestors, that everybody's got the right to have an equal say, and so on and so forth, it's like building our own prison walls. Holding on to these attitudes, we close ourselves off. We tell ourselves that we have no need of the knowledge of the past, of the beliefs of those strange people from way back then. People have this kind of attitude towards Indigenous Australians, for example. Of course they do. How can you take a traditional culture seriously if you believe the modern propaganda about progress, science, contemporary society? You can't. I mean, Indigenous Australians didn't have any of the inventions of the modern age – no mobile phones, no computers, no modern medicine, no feather mattresses – so how can you take them seriously?

In Tibet, a large part of the population was semi-nomadic, and likewise in many other parts of the world. The disappearance of these nomadic peoples in Tibet and in all other corners of the world – throughout Asia, Australia, Africa, the Middle East, North America, everywhere – is a sure sign of the very grave crisis that we're in, because the nomadic peoples represent certain human possibilities, possibilities that are nobler than those we find in sedentary, highly materialised civilizations such as our own. Moreover, the fact that we've actively destroyed them, for that indeed is what we've done whether through open genocide or by various other means, is one of modernity's greatest vandalisms.[1] It is a terrible, terrible thing, even worse than the wanton and criminal destruction of the environment. Many people pay sentimental lip-service to this idea but in their hearts they don't really believe it.

QUESTION: My question is to do with carbon dioxide. Science has found that there are 390 billion tonnes of carbon dioxide in the earth. They found that out by examining the ice at the North and the South Poles, and they've found that since 1930 we've added 200 million tonnes to the atmosphere. They say that if we add another 100 million tonnes, we're in for huge, huge problems. Yet, the United States of America wants to add 1000 billion tonnes to the atmosphere. That's what they plan to do with the situation. It's mad!

HARRY OLDMEADOW: It is. It's completely mad, and it's a good example. We are told that to solve the environmental crisis, we need more science. Now, up to a certain point, that's probably true. Most likely we're not going to get out of this mess now without the help of science in some way, but it's an equally sure thing that science alone will not get us out of this plight. Moreover, left solely to its own devices, science will probably just drive us further into the mess, the reason being that all science can give us is more information, as well as perhaps a certain amount of control. What we need however is not more information, but a different way of understanding the world. Science can't provide this because it is a one-dimensional, horizontal, materialistic, empirical mode of understanding the world.

Plato referred to the Divine qualities of Truth, Beauty, and Goodness. Ask yourself what science can tell us about Truth, Beauty, and Goodness. The answer: nothing! As long as we remain trapped in this kind of modern understanding, further destruction of the environment is inevitable. People think that all of these terrible things that have happened are accidental. They think that really science is a force for good, but that unfortunately we have accidents along the way, and that science is going to fix them. I myself don't think that's how it works at all. The fact that we now have nuclear bombs, that we have cloning, that we have fertilisers that destroy the soil and so on, is not, in my view, accidental. Rather, it's *inevitable*. The laws of karma are inexorable! Given a completely profane science, a science answerable to nothing outside itself, such consequences are inevitable and inescapable.

Q: Is there a way that people can combine these two approaches, even though they look like contradicting philosophy or ideologies? For example, a scientist who follows a certain religion? There are religious people we know of who live by science and by tradition.

HO: Yes, that's true, there are such people and it is possible. Science can find a place within a religious framework. Fine, no problem. But religion cannot be accommodated within a scientific frame. So, sooner or later, one must give one's primary allegiance to one or the other. The problem, I think, is that modern science has become totalitarian. It's taken over the whole field of knowledge, and as a result people now think that if something is scientifically demonstrated then it's true, and if it is not scientifically demonstrated then it's false. Because of this mentality, science gets an open field in which it can do whatever it likes. These days, scientists can do more or less whatever they like, all in the name of advancing scientific knowledge, pushing back the frontiers.

There are several factors at work here. One is the idea of scientific knowledge for its own sake. This is the idea that scientists should be able to get on with their research and do whatever it takes to make further discoveries, and so they have no restraint, no boundaries. There is no one drawing a line, no one saying, look, here's the line and we don't step over this line, because if we do we betray our humanity. I personally think scientists are stepping over this line by pursuing cloning. We shouldn't even be thinking about cloning. We shouldn't even be talking about it! We should affirm from the outset that it is not appropriate behaviour, that we are not so dehumanised that we're going to step over that line. But that is not the case; science is answerable to nobody, except itself, and this is one problem.

Another problem is that an awful lot of science is directed towards profit; it is part of the capitalist machine. A huge number of scientists work for corporations and the bottom line is that they're seeking to make a profit. Another significant part of the scientific establishment is working for the military. So, science is not what it presents itself as; it is not a value-free, objective enquiry into the material world for the benefit of all. That is not what is going on, in my view. No doubt there are many individual scientists who are well-motivated and whose work is beneficial, but, looked at as a whole, I think science is a very dangerous force in the modern world. In this I include all of the technology, modern medicine and so on that are the fruit of science. On the face of it, these things may seem to be beneficial. However, if we step back and consider the whole picture more carefully, we find that it is not that simple. The situation is much more ambiguous than it looks at first sight. For example, we find that many of the "miracle cures" of science are in fact remedies to ailments created by science in the first place. We have no reason to congratulate it on that front! If science hadn't intervened in the first place, the problem wouldn't have arisen and so would not have needed solving.

What's the answer then? The answer is for science to play the kind of role that it plays in traditional societies, which is to say a role where it is not given free rein, where it is answerable to more than itself, and where it takes place within an ethical and epistemological framework provided by religion. If you talk to a professional modern-day scientist, over here at Melbourne University for example, and say, "Now, listen my friend, you must submit yourself to religious authority", you'll get laughed out of the building. No one will take this idea seriously, but this is what we need, I think, because how else is science to be reined in? How is it to be directed towards creative, beneficial ends? It can't produce these out of itself. It's got no wherewithal at all for doing that itself, because there is not and cannot be any wisdom in modern science — it's like a square circle, can't be done.

Q: What if people were to reply, yes, okay, but tell me which religion?

HO: My answer is that it doesn't matter which religion, because all religions, in the end, are essentially the same. As I discussed in "Religion, the Perennial Philosophy, and Traditionalism", all integral religions can offer the sort of guidance that's needed. The situation in the modern West, however, is particularly bad, because science and religion have gone in opposite directions. When did they start doing that? In the Renaissance, that's where the trouble started. Thereafter they started heading off in opposite directions, and they've been at loggerheads, at war, ever since. This is a lamentable situation. On the face of it, we would have to say that science seems to have won. But what kind of victory is it? If the end result is catastrophe, it's no victory at all!

Q: There's a guy in Newcastle University who's written a book about a group of scientists who believe in the Immaculate Conception and the possibility of miracles, but they're modern scientists as well.

HO: This is a something very interesting, and perhaps it is a promising sign as far as science is concerned. For the last four or five hundred years, the scientific understanding of the world has, in a word, been Newtonian. What does that mean? It means that the universe is regarded as a huge empty space within which bits of debris, planets, meteors, and stars, whirl around. It's what's called the Billiard Ball theory of the universe: billiard balls flying around in space and occasionally bumping into each other, with the theory of gravity at play, and so on. We find that, for several hundred years, people have been absolutely convinced that now, through Newtonian physics, they understand the universe as it actually is. But then what happens? The inevitable happens. Someone like Einstein comes along and says, no, that's not how it is. It might appear to be that way, but it's not really that way. And so, with Einstein and the figures who came after him, a whole plethora of theories come about, one after the other: theories of relativity, chaos theory, the uncertainty principle, new physics, string theory, quantum physics and so on and so forth, and lo and behold, what do we discover? We discover, as Frithjof Capra told us in his book[2], that what these new scientists in the field of subatomic physics and so on are discovering – and some of them, poor souls, believe that they're discovering it for the first time – is very much in accord with traditional teachings, whether they be traditional Chinese teachings, traditional Tibetan teachings, traditional Indian teachings, even traditional Western teachings.

What do the scientists say then? They say, "Well, we have now proved and demonstrated that this is indeed how it really is. The people of the past thought that this is how it was, but we've actually proved it." In other words, having discovered a kind of convergence between their own discoveries and what has already been taught in the Vedas, or the ancient Taoist texts, or the Tibetan texts and so on, they don't then reflect and think, "Oh, wouldn't it have been better if we'd given these traditional texts more respect all along?" Instead, they maintain their view that modern science is superior and pompously announce that they have now proven what the people of the past merely suspected, or they say that they've now "verified" what is found in the ancient scriptures. However, it is not up to modern science to verify ancient scriptures; rather, it's the other way around. If we were living in a sane world, we would go about things exactly the other way around, and we wouldn't be surprised that the account we get of time and space in the Vedas, for example, is indeed valid, as far as we can work out through modern science, and that it always has been true, for these thousands of years. It's been true since the beginning, but we don't think of it like that. We think that, until recent times people were hindered by ignorance and superstition, but now, with the advent of modern science, we finally know how it is. It's going to take an awful lot to break through this stubborn shell, these arrogant assumptions of the modern mind, but it absolutely has to be broken through.

Moreover, if we didn't believe in the ideas of progress and evolution, we would have no difficulty with the idea that, in all of the world's different cultures, at different times and in different places, there have been wise people whose understanding of things was deep and true. This is the case and has been the case since 1000 years ago, since 5000 years ago, since 10,000 years ago, and we cannot improve on their understanding and wisdom. Certainly, we might approach it from a different angle and present it in a different way. We might find a new vocabulary, for instance. All of that is fine, but the knowledge itself cannot be improved upon. As I said before, to imagine that we can improve on the teachings of the Buddha is absurd. The teachings are either true or not. As far as I'm concerned, they're true, and they've always been true, and science can neither prove nor disprove them, for the truth of these teachings is inviolate and quite beyond the grasp of profane modes of thought.

Frankly, I'm not even slightly interested in whether science is trying to prove that such teachings are true or not; that is not the business of science. Science sits at a lower level altogether. Religion is the higher value, the greater value, it gives us the fuller understanding. Within the framework of religion, we can have empirical science and other fields of knowledge such as medicine, astronomy, and so forth. That is not a problem at all, when they take place within that framework. However, when you take the framework away and you let those sciences run wild, on their own, the result is the situation we now find ourselves here in the modern world: science run amok, harum-scarum.

Q: There is a scientist called Jeremy Leggett. He worked for an oil company and then started a solar energy company. He gave a talk at the University of New South Wales and it was so touching that I was crying by the end.

HO: That is a hopeful sign, I think, the fact that more and more people trained and working in the field of science are starting to wake up to these larger facts. Take a figure like David Suzuki. A lot of the scientific establishment still just dismiss him. They regard him as a kind of leftover hippie, not to be taken at all seriously. Yet, in spite of that, it does seem that more and more people are starting to see and understand that the whole scientific paradigm has to change. If it doesn't, we are in serious trouble.

Q: I wonder if you could mention some other forces or ideas, outside the world of science, that might indicate that there is hope or faith?

HO: The growing interest in Eastern traditions is tremendously hopeful. There are people all around the Western world, especially young people but not only young people, who are passionately interested in indigenous cultures, Buddhism, Hinduism, Taoism, and in pre-modern Western traditions of one sort or another. This is hopeful because there they have some prospect of finding sustenance for their spiritual hunger. They've woken up to the fact that modern industrial, consumer capitalism is not the answer, not where it's at. They know that life is more than superannuation and salary and status and plasma television sets and whatever else is in fashion at the time. They know this and they know there's something more, something better, something deeper, and they're looking around for it. They might look in the wrong place to begin with and so get confused, but the fact is that they're looking.

The Dalai Lama, to take just one example, must be one of the three or four most widely respected and recognised figures in the entire world, certainly amongst spiritual leaders. This is an extraordinary situation. If we think back to 60 years ago, before the Communist invasion of Tibet, how many people in the Western world would have even heard of the Dalai Lama? Hardly any. How many people would know anything about Tibetan Buddhism? An absolutely negligible number, a few orientalists, explorers, and mountaineers would know a little, but for most ordinary folk it was unheard of. Likewise with the Indian traditions; only a very tiny proportion of the population had any knowledge of such things. But today, walk into any bookshop and you find books by the Dalai Lama, by Chögyam Trungpa, by Shunryu Suzuki and many other Eastern teachers. You find Sufi books, you find traditional Chinese books, books on Indigenous Australian's spirituality, the Kabbalah, the ancient Egyptians. All of these things have become much more accessible and much closer. There's a recognition that these traditions have got something profound to offer. This is an extremely hopeful sign.

QUESTION: Democracy is expanding throughout the world and it looks like it's going to continue to spread farther and wider over the next few hundred years so that more of the world's population will be living in democratic societies. Would you regard this as a hopeful sign?

HARRY OLDMEADOW: Not necessarily. I think this is a very complicated issue. It depends on what the alternative is. As I said before, I agree with Plato that democracy always comes with the danger of tyranny, whether it be the tyranny of the majority, or the tyranny of demagogic leaders. Don't forget that Hitler, for example, was elected to power by a democratic system. He wasn't a military general who seized power by force. Democracy, when you look at it, has a very mixed record. If you were to ask me, do you think it's a good thing that a corrupt and oppressive military junta somewhere is removed and replaced with a democratic system? Of course, of course. As I said earlier, it depends what the alternative is and in the modern world, as Winston Churchill observed, democracy is usually the best of a bad lot of options.

What might be some better alternatives? The kind of alternatives we find in traditional societies. For example, Tibet was essentially a theocracy: spiritual and temporal power was, for the most part, intertwined. It was a system much closer to Plato's Philosopher King model than to democracy, and I'd say that, in principle, that is a better system. However, it's not possible for us to go back to those times. That being so, democracy is probably the best and most viable option in the modern world. Nevertheless, I still think that we need to be careful not to treat democracy as an absolute value, as a self-evident truth that is always the best, because it's not always so. The people don't always know best. That may be the premise of democracy, but at the same time we know that it's not true. Often the people don't know best. I'm more interested in human rights than democracy as such. I think that human rights are tremendously important and must be preserved, but I'm not particularly fussed about the actual form of government, as long as human rights are respected and preserved.

Q: The way I understand democracy is not as a value, but more as a system, a method to achieve the value of human rights.

HO: I agree with you. It's the values, such as human rights, that really matter in the end. The Dalai Lama's position in this regard is, I think, very intelligent. He says that, yes, in an ideal world we would like to go back to Tibet and re-establish things as they previously were. He concedes that there were abuses in Tibet and its governance before the Communist invasion, but he still believes that the previous situation was preferable. At the same time, he takes a very practical approach. He says, if that cannot happen, or since that cannot happen, what then do we need to do? We need to stop violence against the Tibetan people. We need to establish, preserve, and protect human rights in Tibet. We need to stop the destruction of the environment. We need to stop the Sinocization of Tibet. The Dalai Lama strikes a very intelligent balance between preserving tradition and taking account of the political realities of the modern world.

LOOKING FORWARD TO TRADITION

ANCIENT TRUTHS AND MODERN DELUSIONS

...the very idea of tradition has been destroyed to such an extent that those who aspire to recover it no longer know which way to turn.

– René Guénon[1]

In all epochs and all countries there have been revelations, religions, wisdoms; tradition is a part of humankind, just as humanity is part of tradition.

– Frithjof Schuon[2]

66 WHEN A person is tired of London, they is tired of life...",
said Samuel Johnson. Well, ladies and gentlemen, I am tired
of neither. I am very glad to be here. And it is through the good
graces and generosity of the Matheson Trust and the Temenos
Academy that I am so, though I hope you will not hold them
to account for anything I might say tonight. But let us not tarry
over introductions...

Penicillin, computers, man on the moon, Bertrand Russell,
democracy, compulsory education, the United Nations, longer
life expectancy, mobile phones, indoor toilets, anesthetics, Albert
Einstein, the internet, the Genome Project ... a random sample
of the sorts of things which are often marshaled by the apostles of
"Progress". Looking at such a catalogue of apparent marvels one
might be tempted to recall Terry Pratchett's wise dictum that,
"Progress just means bad things happen faster". More seriously,
thinking about the last century some of us might compile a
more sobering and blood-soaked list. For instance: the Somme,
Auschwitz, Hiroshima, serial killers, the Gulag, Chernobyl,
50 million-plus refugees worldwide today, environmental
devastation, terrorism, Pol Pot, Bhopal, pornography as global
mega-business, chemical and biological weapons. Nonetheless,
the idea of "Progress" is one of the most potent shibboleths
of modernity. It comes dressed in many alluring guises, often
hand-in-hand with its shady accomplice, evolutionism, and
finds applications in many fields. So pervasive is this idea in
the modern climate, so much taken for granted, that it has
become almost invisible — rather like the smog to which urban
dwellers become inured. No doubt the unprecedented barbarisms
of the 20th century have caused some disenchantment but the
persistence of the idea is remarkable. "Progress" has a long and
sordid pedigree in Western thought, and many brutalities and

infamies have been justified in its name. To mention just one we might adduce the extirpation of the nomadic cultures, one of the most appalling vandalisms of the last few centuries: Cain's murder of Abel repeats itself on a vast scale. The idea of Progress is modernity's siren song, luring the ways of the past to their destruction. But it is not my purpose tonight to unravel this dark history, nor to analyze the ways in which the pseudo-myth of Progress contaminates almost all aspects of modern thought. In the first instance, I want to focus on an idea which stands at radical odds with it: "Tradition".

TRADITION

"Tradition" has accumulated many unhappy political and sentimental accretions over the last two centuries. Here is Henry Ford, one of the pioneers of industrial mass production:

> I don't know much about history, and I wouldn't give a nickel for all the history in the world. History is more or less bunk. It is tradition. We want to live in the present, and the only history that is worth a tinker's damn is the history we make today.[3]

More often than not nowadays the word "tradition" is used pejoratively, signifying the "dead weight" of the past, useless baggage which should now be jettisoned. Hence Brian Eno, the *avant-garde* musician, tells us that when he returned to England after a year's absence, "the country seemed stuck, dozing in a fairy tale, stifled by the weight of tradition". The English actress, Minnie Driver, declares that, "You do a James Bond film, you're being part of an anachronism, a tradition" — well gosh Minnie, we wouldn't want that![4] For others adherence to "tradition" betrays a mental condition — lazy, conformist, stagnant — as when Jiddu Krishnamurti declares that, "Tradition becomes our security, and when the mind is secure it is in decay" whilst another commentator warns us that, "tradition" is "one of those words conservative people use as a shortcut to thinking".[5] Sometimes the term signals no more than blind custom, or some institution which has persisted over generations but which is now obsolete. Defenders of tradition are associated with a "nostalgia for the past", and perhaps with "romanticism" and "folklore" — sentimental fuddy-duddies with their heads in cloudy idealizations of a Golden Age that never was.[6] Lewis Mumford put the case a little more charitably when he remarked that, "Traditionalists are pessimists about the future and optimists about the past".[7] I prefer to say that it is a matter of neither pessimism nor optimism but of seeing things clearly. I also want to repudiate the conventional notion that we look back on Tradition, belonging to the past, and we look forward to Progress, taking us into the future. Perhaps some of you had the privilege of knowing the late Lord Northbourne. He entitled one of his books *Looking Back on Progress*; in similar vein, and following the suggestion of our Chairman, I entitle this talk "Looking Forward to Tradition". My sub-title is "Ancient Truths and Modern Delusions" which some of you will recognize as an oblique tribute to Martin Lings and his book *Ancient Beliefs and Modern Superstitions*.

Of course, in some quarters, even today, the word "tradition" retains some weight and dignity. Perhaps its most positive usages have been within the discourses of religion and cultural history — and perhaps cricket! Think, for instance, of Dr. Leavis' use of the term when he writes that a literary tradition is "essentially more than an accumulation of separate works: it has an organic form, or constitutes an organic order, in relation to which the individual writer has his [or her] significance".[8] Or recall T.S. Eliot's use of "tradition" to refer to "all those habitual actions, habits, and customs, from the most significant religious rite to our conventional way of greeting a stranger, which represent the blood kinship of 'the same people living in the same place'."[9] Here Eliot renders the term more or less synonymous with "culture" which he defined as "a whole way of life" and "all the characteristic activities and interests of a people".[10] However, no denying that in recent years the word "culture", like "tradition", has been corroded and tarnished by postmodernist theorizing, and by the general "slaughter of the ancestors" conducted by over-heated ideologues and by those Parisian "monks of negation" — Foucault, Derrida et. al.

I want to argue that "tradition", in its full amplitude, is a religious and metaphysical conception and that even its more positive latter-day meanings and associations, as in writers such as Leavis and Eliot, are somewhat restrictive while its more negative usage, as in the postmodernist lexicon, betrays a complete ignorance of what the term might properly comprise. Some seventy years ago, the French metaphysician, René Guénon, observed, "the very idea of tradition has been destroyed to such an extent that those who aspire to recover it no longer know which way to turn"[11] — words certainly no less true today than then!

Guénon's name brings us to one of the central concerns of this talk: the understanding of tradition to be found in a small group of thinkers and writers who have hitherto exerted only a marginal influence on the Anglophone world but whose works unravel some of the darkest enigmas of modernity. Because of the key place occupied in their thought by "tradition"[12] the figures in question have sometimes been referred to as "traditionalists"; another designation is "perennialist".

The traditionalist perspective was first publicly articulated by René Guénon (1886-1951), the remarkable French intellectual (sometimes misleadingly described as an "occultist" and "orientalist") whose metaphysical writings really inaugurate the movement. Since the time of Guénon's first writings, a century ago, a significant traditionalist "school" has emerged with Guénon, Ananda Coomaraswamy (1877-1947) and Frithjof Schuon (1907-1998) recognized as its most authoritative exponents. Other leading figures include Titus Burckhardt, Marco Pallis, Martin Lings and Seyyed Hossein Nasr.[13] These writers are committed to the explication of the Perennial Philosophy which lies at the heart of the diverse religions and behind the manifold forms of the world's different traditions. At the same time, unlike many other so-called perennialists — Aldous Huxley might serve as an example — they are dedicated to the preservation and illumination of the traditional forms which give each religious heritage its distinctive character and guarantee its formal integrity and, by the same token, ensure its spiritual efficacy. In other words they have insisted on the incalculable value of religious orthodoxy.

St Augustine speaks of "Wisdom uncreate, the same now as it ever was and ever will be".[14] This timeless wisdom has carried many names: *Philosophia Perennis*, *Lex Aeterna*, *Hagia Sophia*, *Din al-Haqq*, *Akalika Dhamma* and *Sanatana Dharma* are among the better known. In itself and as such this truth is formless and beyond all conceptualizations. Any attempt to define it is to pursue the wind with a net. This universal wisdom, in existence since the dawn of time and the spiritual patrimony of all humankind, can also be designated as the Primordial Tradition. Guénon refers, in one of his earliest articles, to "the Tradition contained in the Sacred Books of all peoples, a Tradition which in reality is everywhere the same, in spite of all the diverse forms it assumes to adapt itself to each race and period...".[15] In this sense tradition is synonymous with the perennial philosophy itself which is universal and immutable.[16] "Tradition" in its purest metaphysical sense — the sense in which Guénon often means it — signifies the unity of First Principles, an eternal wisdom which, in Schuon's words, signifies "the totality of the primordial and universal truths"[17]. It is one and the same timeless Wisdom which can be found, sometimes heavily veiled, in all the sacred Scriptures, and which nourishes all integral religious traditions. This is a first principle, the *sine qua non* of traditionalist thought. It has met with a good deal of skepticism, even derision, in modern times, which only goes to show how far we have "progressed" in our foolishness. On the other hand, the credibility of the principle, if one might so put it, has also been compromised by a rag-tag of so-called "gurus" and pseudo-spiritual movements claiming adherence to some vague universalist "essence" without really understanding its nature. More often than not such people are shameless iconoclasts who repudiate the very forms in which the perennial wisdom is necessarily clothed; they are also, thereby, anti-traditional.

Schuon and other perennialists point out that all the great religious teachings, albeit in the differing vocabularies appropriate to the spiritual economy in question, affirm a primordial truth or wisdom. We remember Krishna's declaration, in the *Bhagavad Gita*, of the pre-existence of his message, proclaimed at the dawn of time.[18] Likewise Christ, speaking in his cosmic function as Incarnation of the Truth, states, "Verily I say unto you, before Abraham was, I am".[19] Affirmations of the principle are to be found over and over in the religious traditions.[20] "Tradition" in its most pristine sense is this primordial truth and as such takes on the status of a first cause, a cosmic datum, a principial reality woven into the very fabric of the universe. As such it is not amenable to "proof"; it is a self-evident, self-validating principle in the face of which it is possible only to understand or not understand. As Coomaraswamy points out, "a first cause, being itself uncaused, is not probable but axiomatic".[21] Thus the Primordial Tradition or *sophia perennis* is of supra-human origin and is in no sense a product or evolute of human thought: it is "the birth-right of humanity".[22] It is, in Marco Pallis's words, "formless and supra-personal in its essence" and thus "escapes exact definition in terms of human speech and thought". Deploying a Buddhist idiom, Pallis also writes this:

> Only the divine Suchness is unborn and therefore undying, limitless and therefore not limiting, free and therefore the seat of Deliverance. The voice of tradition is the invitation to that freedom whispered in the ear of existential bondage; whatever echoes that message in any degree or at any remove may properly be called traditional; anything that fails to do so, on the other hand, is untraditional and humanistic.[23]

However, the word sometimes carries a different signification which can be confusing. Etymologically "tradition" simply means "that which is transmitted" and this is the key to the second meaning of the word. Here tradition cannot simply be equated with a formless and immutable Truth but is rather that Truth as it finds formal expression, through the medium of a divine Revelation, in the myths, rituals, doctrines, iconographies and other manifestations of different primal and religious civilizations. The Truth as such is formless and so cannot be conveyed, *as such*, within forms: thus it is aspects of Truth or, we might say, partial truths or intimations which are transmitted by traditional forms.[24] Thirdly, "tradition" may sometimes refer to the living process of the transmission itself. Lastly it may also refer to the channels of transmission. This is not as confusing as it might look: once the distinction between the first sense and the other three has been grasped then the meaning is signalled by the context in which it is used.

When Guénon uses the word "tradition" he is more often than not referring to the primordial wisdom as such; he was not much interested in history in general, nor in the annals of the particular religions. However, later perennialists frequently use the word "traditions" to refer to different religious and spiritual heritages as they are manifested in time, conduits for the transmission of truths of supra-human origin, couched in the forms which have been providentially adapted to suit the needs and receptivities of the peoples and civilizations in question. Tradition, then, entails "an effective communication of principles of more-than-human origin... through use of forms that will have arisen by applying those principles to contingent needs."[25]

Plainly tradition here means vastly more than the observance of custom; it cannot be understood as a mere temporal continuity nor assimilated to any historical process. As Brian Keeble has observed:

> ...tradition is far beyond being merely an accumulation of human endeavour and invention even if it does have a history. Granting that the external characteristics and expression of a tradition are coloured by and reflect the passage of time, nonetheless, to equate tradition with a form of historical continuity is to ignore its supra-formal essence in the name

of which it remains free and objective in relation to spatio-temporal determinations.[26]

As Guénon insisted, "there is nothing and can be nothing truly traditional that does not contain some elements of a superhuman order."[27] In our context, then, the term cannot be applied to anything of purely human provenance — which is to say most of modern culture, even if traces of fossilized traditional forms inevitably persist. It must always be remembered, to cite Brian Keeble again, that:

> Tradition cannot be improvised from human means for by the terms of a tradition the human state as such is by definition a mode of ignorance — a blindness that cannot, by merely having recourse to itself, overcome its own unknowingness.[28]

On the other hand, tradition cannot simply be equated with religion which is one form of tradition, neither exclusive nor exhaustive. Thus "tradition" is more inclusive than "religion" though the relationship of the latter to the former is always intimate. A tradition may appear in a guise which cannot strictly be termed "religious", this word implying the presence of certain formal elements which may be missing. A tradition may, for instance, be embedded in a complex of stories and rituals which might more properly be described as mythological rather than religious. Or again, one might refer to an esoteric wisdom which may be associated with religious forms but which is distinct from them — one can speak, for example, of the Pythagorean or the alchemical tradition. However, these qualifications not-withstanding, in most cases where the word "tradition" is used in a perennialist context the writer has in mind a religious tradition including, of course, whatever esoteric currents might be associated with it. This is to say that tradition here encompasses more than the visible exoteric forms.

Marco Pallis provides us with a kind of working definition of a religious tradition:

> ...wherever a complete tradition exists [he writes] this will entail the presence of four things, namely: a source of... Revelation; a current of influence or Grace issuing from that source and transmitted without interruption through a variety of channels; a way of "verification" which, when faithfully followed, will lead the human subject to successive positions where he is able to "actualize" the truths that Revelation communicates; finally there is the formal embodiment of tradition in the doctrines, arts, sciences and other elements that together go to determine the character of a normal civilization.[29]

Revelation, grace, method, forms: these are the four indispensable constituents of any religious tradition properly so-called.

What then is a traditional civilization? In *Notes towards the Definition of Culture* (1948) Eliot posed the question:

> whether what we call the culture, and what we call the religion of a people are not different aspects of the same thing: the culture being essentially the incarnation (so to speak) of the religion of a people.[30]

The great scholar of Jewish mysticism, Gershom Scholem, has written that tradition "embodies the realization of the effectiveness of the Word in every concrete state and relationship entered into by a society."[31] For perennialists, tradition is the "application and full extension in every domain" of Revelation.[32] Thus the Revelation informs the arts and crafts, the sciences and the social life of a traditional civilization, as well as its theology and spiritual means. In this sense, then, tradition is "the chain that joins civilization to Revelation"[33] and "the mediator between time and eternity".[34] As Seyyed Hossein Nasr insists:

> Tradition is inextricably related to revelation and religion, to the sacred, to the notion of orthodoxy, to authority, to the continuity and regularity of transmission of the truth, to the exoteric and the esoteric as well as to the spiritual life, science and the arts.[35]

Of the many formal elements which necessarily appear in any tradition the perennialists have paid especially close attention to sacred art. We might note in passing the implications of Schuon's affirmation that, "Traditions appear out of the Infinite like flowers; they can no more be invented than can the sacred art which is their witness and their proof."[36]

This view of tradition has all manner of implications and applications. Let us consider a few. The traditionalists, unlike most modern social theorists, find no absolute or self-evident value in "society" as such, nor, indeed, in what is called "civilization". Nor are they susceptible to the "demagogic obsession with purely 'social' values" which is nowadays so widespread, even amongst believers".[37] As Schuon points out:

> When people talk about "civilization" they generally attribute a qualitative meaning to the term, but really civilization only represents a value provided it is supra-human in origin and implies for the civilized man a sense of the sacred...A sense

of the sacred is fundamental for every civilization because fundamental for man; the sacred — that which is immutable, inviolable, and so infinitely majestic — is in the very substance of our spirit and of our existence.[38]

Traditional societies are grounded in an awareness of this reality. Society itself represents nothing of absolute value except insofar as it provides a context for the sense of the sacred and the spiritual life which it implies.[39]

Such a vision of a religious culture is radically opposed to the Marxist/Durkheimian thesis about the relationship between religion and society. It is not society which fashions religion in its own image but religion which shapes the society whose whole rationale is embedded in the sense of which Schuon speaks. In traditional societies, "It is the spiritual, not the temporal, which culturally, socially and politically is the criterion of all other values."[40] It is from this platform that the traditionalists reaffirm the values of civilizations other than our own and from which the most trenchant critique of modernity can be mounted. Western civilization is now, in Guénon's words, "devoid of any traditional character with the exception of the religious element",[41] which itself is increasingly devastated on all sides. Such an understanding also disallows those condescending, sometimes frankly contemptuous, attitudes to the past widespread today amongst so many of the so-called "intelligentsia".

A tradition is not static, an unchanging datum that persists in a frozen state through time. Traditions are dynamic: if needs be, they can grow, branch out and blossom. However, the principle of continuity which preserves the link with the Revelation must always be respected if the tradition is to remain an integral one. As G.K. Chesterton pithily remarked, tradition "does not mean that the living are dead but that the dead are alive".[42] "The growth of a tradition," writes Titus Burckhardt, "resembles that of a crystal, which attracts homologous particles to itself, incorporating them according to its own laws of unity."[43] In the final phrase ("its own laws of unity") we find the key to the principle of orthodoxy. The great doctrinal formulations which follow a Revelation, usually at some historical distance, do not, essentially, constitute an "addition" to the tradition but an unfolding of principles and perspectives which until then have remained implicit. One thinks of a Shankara, a Nagarjuna, an Aquinas, an Ibn 'Arabi or the Sixth Patriarch. Such figures disavow any personal "originality", claiming only to be elaborating the spiritual teaching to which they are heirs. Burckhardt again: "Doctrine grows, not so much by addition of new knowledge, as by the need to refute errors and to reanimate a diminishing power of intuition...".[44] For the traditionalists there is always something providential about the appearance of the great doctors of theology and metaphysics.[45]

MODERNITY

Let me now turn briefly to a few remarks about modernity which in the European context means the post-medieval era inaugurated by the Renaissance and subsequently shaped by the Scientific Revolution, the so-called Enlightenment, and the economic and political upheavals and transformations of the 19th century. Our interest here is primarily in what, for want of a better word, we might call "modernism"[46] — the dominant worldview of the post-medieval West. One might classify the ingredients of modernism under any number of schema. Lord Northbourne typifies modernism as "anti-traditional, progressive, humanist, rationalist, materialist, experimental, individualist, egalitarian, free-thinking and intensely sentimental".[47] Seyyed Hossein Nasr gathers these tendencies together under four general features of modern thought: anthropomorphism (and by extension, secularism); evolutionist progressivism; the absence of any sense of the sacred; an unrelieved ignorance of metaphysical principles.[48] Frithjof Schuon observes that:

> ...humanistic culture, insofar as it functions as an ideology and therefore as a religion, consists essentially in being unaware of three things: firstly, of what God is, because it does not grant primacy to Him; secondly, of what man is, because it puts him in place of God; thirdly, of what the meaning of life is, because this culture limits itself to playing with evanescent things and to plunging into them with criminal unconsciousness.[49]

Modernism is a disease which continues to spread like a plague across the globe, destroying traditional cultures wherever they are still to be found. Although its historical origins are European, modernism is now tied to no specific area or civilization. Its symptoms can be detected in a wide assortment of inter-related mind sets and -isms, sometimes involved in cooperative co-existence, sometimes engaged in apparent antagonism, but always united by the same underlying assumptions. Scientism, rationalism, relativism, materialism, positivism, empiricism, evolutionism, psychologism, individualism, humanism, existentialism— these are some of the prime follies of modernist thought, and they are all variations on a theme. Their genealogy can be traced back through a series of intellectual and cultural upheavals in European history to certain vulnerabilities in Christendom which left it exposed to the subversions of a profane science. The Renaissance, the Scientific Revolution and the Enlightenment were all incubators of ideas and values which first ravaged Europe and then spread throughout the world like a lethal virus. Behind the bizarre array of ideologies which have proliferated in the last few centuries we can discern a growing and persistent ignorance concerning ultimate realities and an indifference, if not always an overt hostility, to the eternal verities of Tradition. Not without reason did William Blake characterize the modern worldview as "Single Vision", a flat, horizontal understanding of reality which strips the "outer" world of its mystery, its grandeur and its revelatory function, and which denies our human vocation. As he so acutely remarked, "Man is either the ark of God or a phantom of the earth and the water".[50] In similar vein, W.B. Yeats penned that now well-known passage, "The mischief began at the end of the seventeenth century when man became passive before a mechanized nature...Soul must become its own betrayer, its own deliverer, the one activity, the mirror turn lamp".[51]

Since the Scientific Revolution of the 17th century the prevailing worldview amongst the Western intelligentsia (and alas, increasingly elsewhere) has been constructed on the foundations of scientism — which is to say on an ideology, albeit one heavily camouflaged in the sterilized vestments of "scientific objectivity". Science (a field and method of inquiry) becomes scientism (an ideology) when it refuses to acknowledge the limits of its own competence, denies the authority of any sources which lie outside its ambit, and lays claim to a comprehensive validity as if it could explain no matter what, and as if it were not contradictory to lay claim to totality on an empirical basis. (Witness Stephen Hawking's preposterous pretensions to a "Theory of Everything" or the grandiose claims made on behalf of the Genome Project!) Although this ideology has come under the most cogent criticism from many directions it retains its grip on the modern mentality and its spokesmen are increasingly strident and arrogant in their triumphalism. So it is, for example, that Richard Dawkins can assert, "It is absolutely safe to say that if you meet anybody who claims not to believe in evolution that person is ignorant, stupid or insane".[52] Thanks for that Richard! So pervasive is the scientistic regime that the American National Science Foundation can asseverate, with hardly a murmur of dissent from anywhere, that, "Science extends and enriches our lives, expands our imagination and liberates us from the bonds of ignorance and superstition." Such bromides are to be found all around us. Yet, as David Berlinsky observes, "there is hardly any reason to believe them to be true".[53] We might well recall Gai Eaton's remark that the so-called advance of science is a matter of "knowing more and more about less and less". Modern science, to be sharply distinguished from what the ancients called natural philosophy, is today effectively inseparable from scientism. That this kind of science — and we can find hardly any other, in the Western world at least — might constrict and impoverish our lives, stifle our imaginations and imprison us in both ignorance and superstition, is a proposition which will strike most people as self-evidently absurd.

Some years ago E.F. Schumacher observed that:

> Nothing is more conducive to the brutalization of the modern world than the launching of, in the name of science, wrongful and degraded definitions of man, such as "the naked ape". What could one expect from such a creature...?[54]

Thanks to the likes of Richard Dawkins such definitions are now more widely countenanced than ever, at least amongst the so-called intellectual elites. Berlinsky observes that it is an article of faith amongst the belligerent atheists that humankind is no more than another biological species, enmeshed in the Darwinian struggle for survival:

> The thesis that we are all nothing more than vehicles for a number of "selfish genes" has accordingly entered deeply into the simian gabble of academic life, where together with materialism and moral relativism it now seems...self-evident...[55]

The same might be said of many of the other bleak reductionistic accounts of the human being which litter modern thought. Reductionism, to recall Kathleen Raine's vivid image, is that habit of mind "which sees in the pearl nothing but the disease of the oyster".[56]

No one will deny that modernity has its compensations, though these are often of a quite different order from the loudly trumpeted "benefits" of science and technology — some of which are indubitable but many of which issue in consequences far worse than the ills which they are apparently repairing. Furthermore, many so-called "advances" must be seen as the poisoned fruits of a Faustian bargain which must one day come to its bitter conclusion. What indeed is a man profited if he gain the whole world but lose his own soul? In this context we might remind ourselves of Schuon's caution that:

> When the modern world is contrasted with traditional civilizations, it is not simply a question of seeking the good things and the bad things on one side or the other; good and evil are everywhere, so that it is essentially a question of knowing on which side the more important good and on which side the lesser evil is to be found. If someone says that

such and such a good exists outside tradition, the answer is: no doubt, but one must choose the most important good, and it is necessarily represented by tradition; and if someone says that in tradition there exists such and such an evil, the answer is: no doubt, but one must choose the lesser evil, and again it is tradition that embodies it. It is illogical to prefer an evil which involves some benefits to a good which involves some evils.[57]

On the other hand, one real advantage of living in these latter days is the ready access we have to the spiritual treasuries of the world's religious and mythological traditions, including esoteric teachings which have hitherto been veiled in secrecy.

If we are to believe the textbooks the story of the modern world is one of man's climb out of a dark world of ignorance, superstition and barbarism into a more spacious and sunlit world wherein we understand how things really stand and in which, with the aid of science and reason, we can determine our own destiny. But as Blake and Yeats so well understood, the modern understandings of the human condition have actually reduced and imprisoned us. Is it not one of the most galling ironies of modernity that these much vaunted ideologies and scientific theorizations which, we are told *ad nauseam*, have emancipated us from "the shackles of ignorance and superstition", have, in reality robbed us of all that is most precious in the human estate "hard to obtain", by denying the Divine Spark which we all carry within? This, truly speaking, is a monstrous crime against God and thereby against humanity.

Many of the luminaries of modern though — from Darwin and Marx, through Nietzsche and Freud, down to the Parisian postmodernists — deprive man of his fundamental freedom by portraying him as the subject of blind, impersonal forces: in

Darwin's case the biological imperatives of the survival of the fittest; for Marx, the dialectic of the material forces of history; for Freud the sexual drive with all its accompanying repressions, projections, complexes and neuroses; for Nietzsche, the "will to power". In each case we are offered a meagre and charmless portrait of the human condition: man as biological organism, as a highly evolved ape whose essential function is to ensure the survival of the species, and whose behaviour is governed by the iron dictates of biological necessity; man as economic animal, fashioned by his material environment and by the impersonal forces of history; man as a herd-creature, mediocre, cowardly, foolish and deluded, redeemed only by the *Übermensch* who dares to exercise the will to power; the human being as a marionette of the dark forces of the Id. As Guénon so acutely observed nearly a century ago, "While nineteenth century materialism closed the mind of man to what is above him, twentieth century psychology opened it to what is below him".[58] But it hardly matters whether these purportedly scientific accounts be of a pseudo-biological, psychological or sociological nature, not to mention the surreal postmodernist "erasure" of the human individual altogether! These are all variations on a single theme — man cut off from the transcendent, a creature living in an entirely horizontal world, a puppet of "drives", "complexes", "reflexes", "conditionings", and "historical forces".

It comes as no surprise that each of these thinkers leaves God out of the frame. In the case of Marx, Freud and Nietzsche, the disavowal is quite explicit whilst in Darwin it is a matter of ignoring the question, which amounts to more or less the same thing. The transcendent dimension of both the cosmos and the microcosmic human being is stripped away to leave us in an entirely horizontal world in which there is no longer any sense of our dignity, responsibility and freedom as the children of God. In such a world there is no longer any sense of the sacred from which we might take our spiritual bearings. Our souls cry out for bread but we are given stones. It might also be said that these God-denying thinkers paved the road to the slaughter-houses of the 20th century. We now better understand the truth of Dostoevsky's frightful premonition that "without God, everything is permitted".

The modern mentality is rationalistic, materialistic, empiricist, historicist and humanistic. The adulation of Reason and of an empirical and materialistic science could only arise in a world in which the sacred sciences of the traditional worlds had been lost. To cleave to these much-vaunted modes of modern thought is simply to announce that one is entirely bereft of any metaphysical discernment, entrapped in the world of maya, that tissue of fugitive relativities which makes up the time-space world. As Frithjof Schuon has tersely remarked, "The rationalism of a frog living at the bottom of a well is to deny the existence of mountains; this is logic of a kind, perhaps, but it has nothing to do with reality".[59] To succumb to the idolatry of Reason is also, necessarily, to turn one's back on the ever-present sources of traditional intellectuality and spirituality, which is to say doctrine and spiritual method — the epochal Revelations providentially directed towards various human collectivities, the traditions issuing from these Revelations, the Scriptures and commentaries of the doctors and sages of each tradition, the witness of the saints and mystics. All this is thrown out in favour of the prejudices of the day, largely fashioned by those pseudo-mythologies current at any particular moment.[60] Forget Lao Tzu, forget Meister Eckhart, forget Ramana Maharshi — listen instead to Bertrand Russell or Christopher Hitchens or

Sam Harris: can a more bizarre and ludicrous proposition be imagined?

OUR CONTEMPORARY PREDICAMENT

I started this talk with reference to the pseudo-mythology of Progress: the absurdity of progressivism, if one may so call it, is exposed by the most cursory consideration of our contemporary situation. Who can deny that there is indeed a fundamental crisis in the modern world and that its root causes are spiritual. The crisis itself can hardly be disputed. Some of the symptoms: ecological catastrophe, a material sign of the rupture between Heaven and Earth; a rampant materialism and consumerism, signifying a surrender to the illusion that man can live by bread alone; the genocidal extirpation of traditional cultures by the careering juggernauts of "modernization"; political barbarities on an almost unimaginable scale; social discord, endemic violence and dislocations of unprecedented proportions; widespread alienation, ennui and a sense of spiritual sterility amidst the frenetic confusion and din of modern life; a religious landscape dominated by internecine and inter-religious strife and by the emergence of bellicose fundamentalisms in both East and West; the loss of any sense of the sacred, even among those who remain committed to religious forms, many of whom have retreated into a credulous religious literalism or into a vacuous liberalism where "anything goes". These signs of the times — and the inventory is by no means exhaustive — are plain enough to those with eyes to see. No amount of gilded rhetoric about "progress", the "miracles of modern science and technology", or the "triumphs of democracy" (to mention just three of modernity's "sacred cows") can hide the fact that our age is tyrannized by an outlook inimical to our most fundamental needs, our deepest yearnings, our most noble aspirations. As Frithjof Schuon has acutely observed:

> That which is lacking in the present world is a profound knowledge of the nature of things; the fundamental truths are always there, but they do not impose themselves because they cannot impose themselves on those unwilling to listen.[61]

Those truths, so often derided in the modern world, can be found in Tradition — and as I hope I have made clear, by this term we mean something very different from the jaundiced senses it has accumulated in the modern mentality. We must dispel the false charges sometimes leveled at traditionalists that they are dusty obscurantists "out of touch" with the contemporary world, that they want to "wind back the clock", that they are romantic reactionaries escaping into an idealized past. Let us never forget that the essential message of tradition is timeless and thus ever new, ever fresh, and always germane to both our immediate condition and to our ultimate destiny. As Schuon remarks, a "nostalgia for the past" is, in itself, nothing; all that is meaningful is "a nostalgia for the sacred" which "cannot be situated elsewhere than in the liberating 'now' of God".[62] In this sense we do not look back to Tradition as a relic of the past: we look forward to re-discovering those ever-present intellectual and spiritual treasures vouchsafed by Tradition. From another point of view we might say that we must look neither backwards nor forwards but upwards. And here, by way of an aside, we might note that one of the roots and symptoms of a horizontal worldview is historicism — that mentality which holds that everything is to be explained by the exigencies and vicissitudes of Time. For such a mentality there can be no looking up.[63]

No doubt our crepuscular era is riddled with all manner of confusions but there are many directions in which we can still turn to find a way out of the darkness. It might be through humble listening and dialogue with those representatives of authentic traditional forms such as still survive in the modern world, or through the lessons of the primordial cultures of the nomadic and indigenous peoples. We can turn to the saints and sages who are always in our midst, though often hidden from view, and without whom the world would instantly vanish: in recent times one might mention such figures as the Algerian Sufi master, Shaykh Ahmed Al Alawi, or Hindu sages such as Paramahamsa Ramakrishna, Ramana Maharshi and Anandamayi, or Native American visionaries such as Black Elk and Chief Thomas Yellowtail, not to mention the many wise lamas and masters of the Far Eastern world. We can turn to the example and writings of those Christian writers who can help us discover anew the spiritual treasures which are close at hand but often forgotten or obscured — I am thinking of figures such as Thomas Merton, Bede Griffiths, and the French monk, Henri Le Saux who became Swami Abhishiktananda. Then, too, there is the abiding work and example of the great perennialists of whom I have made mention in this talk. At a time when the forces of anti-Tradition sometimes seem overwhelming and when we feel unable to keep our hands to the plough, let us recall Frithjof Schuon's reminder that no effort on behalf of the Truth is ever in vain.[64] Before inviting you to ask me questions which I cannot answer I will conclude this talk, as I have done others, with some salutary words from René Guénon:

Those who might be tempted to give way to despair should realize that nothing accomplished in this order can ever be lost, that confusion, error and darkness can win the day only apparently and in a purely ephemeral way, that all partial and transitory disequilibrium must perforce contribute towards the great equilibrium of the whole, and that nothing can ultimately prevail against the power of truth. Their watchword should be that used formerly by certain initiatory organizations of the West : *Vincit Omnia Veritas.*[65]

Thank you. Peace be with you!

Boudnath Stupa, Kathmandu, Nepal.

The Jade Buddha for Universal Peace, The Great Stupa of Universal
Compassion, Bendigo, Australia.

Guru Rinpoche
(Padmasambhava), who
revealed the Vajyarana which
inaugugrated the The Tibetan
Buddhist tradition, The Great
Stupa of Universal Compassion,
Bendigo, Australia

Buddha figures, Swayambunath Stupa, Kathmandu, Nepal

119

ON FRITHJOF SCHUON'S

TREASURES OF BUDDHISM[1]

The Buddha is renunciation, peace, mercy, and mystery. Mystery is the essence of truth which cannot be adequately conveyed through language but which may suddenly be made plain in an illuminating flash through a symbol, such as a key word, a mystic sound, or an image whose suggestive action may be scarcely graspable.

– Frithjof Schuon

T REASURES OF *Buddhism* could only have come from the sovereign metaphysician of our era, "one of the greatest exponents ever of the perennial wisdom;...one who is equally at home — and in a masterly fashion — in all of its many and varied and historic forms".[2] This compilation of Frithjof Schuon's essays on Buddhist themes provides a conspectus that fully respects but transcends the exoteric religious understandings of the various schools and branches of this great tradition. It presents a peerless exposition of many particular doctrines, symbols, and rites as well as illuminating the nature of Shinto and its relation to Buddhism. Furthermore, and most importantly, it brings Buddhism to the reader as a living spiritual force.

Along the way the author banishes many misunderstandings that are widespread in the West amongst both the advocates and opponents of what is understood to be "Buddhism". Consider the salutary remarks opening the chapter "Originality of Buddhism":

> Whoever sets out to define a spiritual phenomenon situated in the still quasi-heavenly era of the great Revelations has to beware of assessing it according to the impoverishing "categories" of a later age or, still worse, those belonging to the completely profane "free-thinking" world. Buddhism, which is so often reduced to the level of a base philosophical empiricism, has in fact nothing to do with an ideology that is purely human and thus devoid of any enlightening or salvific quality; to deny the celestial character of Shakyamuni and his Message is tantamount to saying that there can be effects without a cause, and this remark applies moreover for all *Avatāras* and all sacred institutions (p. 15).

The status of this tradition, so to speak, is a subject that has caused untold confusion — amongst the adherents of other religions, amongst those who champion atheism and agnosticism, amongst many Western converts, and even, in these later times, amongst practitioners within the Buddhist homelands whose thinking has been adulterated by modern influences. No doubt these misapprehensions arise from many sources, but four are readily apparent: firstly, from a Hindu vantage-point Buddhism presents itself as a heterodoxy; secondly, Buddhism is problematic in the perspective of any exoteric theism; thirdly, the spiritual methodology of Buddhism rests on the metaphysic of the Void, misunderstood as a kind of nihilism of which the doctrine of "no soul" (*anattā*) is seen as another scandalous instance; lastly, many Westerners attracted to Buddhism, often unaware of its close affinities with the Christian tradition which they have repudiated, laud it as "rational", "empirical", "scientific", "humanistic", and the like, and disavow its religious "trappings". They sometimes claim that Buddhism is a "way of life" or a "philosophy" rather than a "religion". What does Frithjof Schuon say about these matters?

On the question of Buddhism's relation to the Hindu tradition out of which it emerged:

> The first question to be asked concerning a doctrine or tradition is that of its intrinsic orthodoxy; that is to say one must know whether this tradition is in conformity, not necessarily with another given traditionally orthodox perspective, but simply with Truth. As far as Buddhism is concerned, we will not ask therefore whether it agrees with the letter of the *Veda* or if its "non-theism" — and not "atheism" — can be reconciled in its expression with Semitic theism or any other, but simply

whether Buddhism is true in itself; which means, if the answer is in the affirmative, that it will agree with the Vedic spirit and that its "non-theism" will express the Truth — or a sufficient and efficacious aspect of this Truth — whereof theism provides another possible expression, opportune for the world it rules (p. 16).

No doubt, from a certain viewpoint, Buddhism might be understood as a reaction against various excesses, corruptions, and degenerations within the Brahmanical tradition, just as Christianity can be seen as a reaction against Judaic legalism and pharisaism. But to think of the Buddha as a "reformer" is to misunderstand him and his message. The Buddha is "renunciation, peace, mercy, and mystery", the last being "the essence of truth, which cannot be adequately articulated through language" (p. 10). As to Shankara's refutation of Buddhism, this, precisely, "does not show why Buddhism is false but why Hinduism cannot admit it without nullifying itself" (p. 181).

On the vexed question of Buddhism's non-theism and its "negative" metaphysic, Schuon writes that:

> If one accepts that "the kingdom of Heaven is within you", then one cannot logically reproach Buddhism for conceiving the Divine Principle in this respect alone. The "Void" or "Extinction" is God — the supra-ontological Real and Being seen "inwardly" — within ourselves; not in our thought or in our ego, of course, but starting from that "geometrical point" within us whereby we are mysteriously linked to the Infinite. Buddhist "atheism" consists in a refusal to objectivize or exteriorize the "God within" in a dogmatic form (p. 19).

Buddhism's non-theism, its emphasis on "the mystery of immanence" (p. 188), is one expression amongst many of the Truth, one that is not only possible but necessary:

> Buddhism, inasmuch as it is a characteristic perspective and independently of its modes, is necessary: it could not but come to be, given that a non-anthropomorphic, impersonal, and "static" consideration of the Infinite is in itself a possibility; such a perspective had therefore to be manifested at a particular cyclical moment and in a human setting that rendered it opportune, for the existence of a given receptacle calls for that of a given content (pp. 16-17).

Moreover, Buddhism is "a 'Hinduism universalized', just as Christianity and Islam — each in its own way — are a Judaism rendered universal, hence separated from its particular ethnic milieu and made accessible to people hailing from all origins" (p. 17). Whilst it is true that Buddhism rests on a metaphysic which is not essentially different to that of the Vedanta, it would be a grave mistake to infer that thereby it "does not represent just as spontaneous and autonomous a reality as do the other great Revelations" (p. 17). Dialectically and methodically, it is founded on the experience of human suffering; it is a spiritual way directed to the cessation of such suffering:

> the doctrines of the Buddhas are only "celestial mirages" intended to catch, as in a golden net, the greatest possible number of creatures plunged in ignorance, suffering, and transmigration, and that it is therefore the benefit of creatures and not the suchness of the Universe that determines the necessarily contingent form of the Message; . . . and secondly,

because Buddhism, within the framework of its own wisdom, goes beyond the formal "mythology" or the "letter" and ultimately transcends all possible human formulations, thus realizing an unsurpassable contemplative disinterestedness as do the Vedanta, Taoism, and analogous doctrines (p. 87).

It follows that the claims sometimes made by Orientalists and Western converts that Buddhism is simply a "philosophy" or "natural religion" have more to say about modern prejudices than about Buddhism properly understood.

Buddhism comprises an immense spiritual universe in which we find an encyclopedic range of religious forms and practices, evident in the very different inflections given to the Buddha's saving message in the Theravada, *Vajrayāna*, Zen, and Pure Land branches of the tradition. On these great branches and their various schools and sects, Schuon has written with characteristic percipience. The author moves freely through "the vast and varied extension" (p. 25) of the Buddhist world, sometimes taking a lofty overview, at others focusing sharply on a particular subject — but always attuned to both the universal and the distinctive features of this tradition. We need hardly add that the author is immune to those modernist prejudices that have marred so much of the Western literature on Buddhism. Schuon's writings are all the more illuminating, and sometimes startling, given that Buddhism has received comparatively little attention within the perennialist school inaugurated by René Guénon, but given its fullest and most authoritative expression by the author of the present volume. No less a figure than Guénon himself for many years harbored the notion that Buddhism was no more than a Hindu heterodoxy until he was set right by Ananda Coomaraswamy and Marco Pallis, who, after Schuon, are the two foremost perennialist authorities on this tradition.

It only remains to make a few passing remarks about Shinto, the mythological and shamanistic Japanese tradition which can readily be included in a book such as this because "Japanese civilization can be said to stem, both structurally and in its particular genius, from the synthesis between Shinto and Buddhism" (p. 137). Firstly, it is as well to disown the common supposition that Shinto ancestorism replaced the Divinity with the ancestors, which overlooks the fact that "the Divinity itself is conceived in the Far East as a kind of Ancestor, and one's human ancestors are like a prolongation of the Divinity, or like a bridge between ourselves and it" (p. 141). It is for this reason that "the ancestor is at once the origin and the spiritual or moral norm":

> he is, for his descendants, the essential personality, that is to say the substance of which they are like the accidents; and piety consists precisely in viewing him thus and in seeing in him but the bridge connecting them — his descendants — with the Divine. . . Ancestors are the human imprints of angelic substances and, for that reason, also of divine Qualities; to be true to them is to be true to God (pp. 142-143).

The cult of the Emperor is a particular expression of the same principle.

The spiritual affinities between Shinto and other forms of "Hyperborean Shamanism" are manifest in "many mythological, cultural, and even vestimentary similarities", in the cult of Nature, and, amongst their practitioners, in "their thirst for freedom, their contempt for luxury, their taciturnity, and other similar characteristics" (pp. 143-144); the comparisons with the American Indians are too obvious to need laboring. These affinities also go to explain why Shinto was so easily able to assimilate Far Eastern forms of Buddhism (especially the ideal of the Bodhisattva), also remembering that "The passage from one Asiatic tradition to another — Hinduism, Buddhism, Taoism — is a small thing, seeing that the metaphysical content is everywhere clearly apparent".[3]

ON MARCO PALLIS' *THE WAY AND THE MOUNTAIN*

One can truly say that this remote land [Tibet] behind the snowy
rampart of the Himalaya had become like the chosen sanctuary for all
those things whereof the historical discarding had caused our present
profane civilization, the first of its kind, to come into being...

– Marco Pallis

T HE RECENT history of Tibet exemplifies the fate of traditional civilizations in the modern world. Behind the snowy ramparts of the Himalayas, Tibet had stood as one of the last bastions of a way of life which properly deserved to be called traditional — one directed, in the first place, not to a godless ideal of material "progress" but to the spiritual welfare of its people, a culture which, in T.S. Eliot's phrase, was an incarnation of the religious outlook which informed it. In a sense, Tibet served as a haven for all those principles and ideals, all those aspirations of the human spirit, which were elsewhere being trampled underfoot by the forces of modernity. That the invasion of Tibet and the destruction of its religious culture should be carried out by its neighbour in the name of a profane Western ideology is one of the most bitter ironies of recent history. Let us not mince words: the systematic subversion of Tibet's religious heritage, the slaughter of its monks and nuns, the sacking of the monasteries, the unceasing violation of human rights, the cynical "population policy" to make Tibetans a minority in their own land, and the desecration of the environment, make the Chinese occupation an imperial vandalism no less appalling than that of the Western powers in so many different parts of the globe in the preceding century.

There are those who make much of the various social abuses and corruptions which, as the present Dalai Lama has conceded, were to be found in Tibet on the eve of the Chinese invasion, as if these could in any measure justify the monstrous brutalities which were to follow. On the other hand, there is nothing to be gained from that sentimental romanticism and nostalgia for the exotic which paints traditional Tibet as a pristine Utopia. Marco Pallis did not fall into either trap. In an Appendix to *Peaks and Lamas* and in his Foreword to Chögyam Trungpa's

Born in Tibet he acknowledged various ills in traditional Tibet and situated them in the proper context. No one with any sense of proportion can for a moment doubt that the good in Tibet's traditional civilization far outweighed the bad, and that something infinitely precious and irreplaceable was destroyed forever by the invading juggernaut.

The peculiar character of Tibetan civilization stemmed from the creative fusion of the indigenous shamanistic tradition of Bön-po with the Mahayana Buddhism brought to Tibet by Padmasambhava and the monks of India. From this spiritual intercourse sprang forth the *Vajrayāna*, that luminous form of Buddhism which expressed the religious genius of the Tibetan people and which seemed to draw its inspiration from the austere and awesome beauty of Tibet's majestic peaks and vast plateaus. Here, preserved in the monastic lineages and in the customs and institutions of the people, was to be found a spiritual treasury of almost incomparable beauty and richness. We need think no further than the ideal of the Bodhisattva and its resplendent iconography, of Chenrezig, Tara and Manjushri, of Milarepa, of the long line of Dalai Lamas who embody the ideal of Wisdom-Compassion which lies at the very heart of the tradition.

Marco Pallis (1895-1989), an author, mountaineer and musician of Greek and British background, was one of a small group of Westerners who had the privilege of experiencing the traditional culture of Tibet in its eventide, visiting the Himalayan regions in 1923, 1933, 1936 and 1947. He was drawn there by his love of mountaineering and, no doubt, by impulses which at the time he himself could only sense as through a glass darkly. So profound was the impact of his early visits that by the mid-1930s Pallis had become a committed dharma-practitioner and an initiated member of one of the Tibetan orders. Thenceforth he was to be one of the most eloquent witnesses of the calamity which afflicted his spiritual homeland, one of a small handful of Westerners who alerted the rest of the world to the magnitude of the tragedy which was unfolding in Tibet. He also devoted himself to the explication of Tibetan religious and cultural forms which were still so little understood in the West. At a time when all too many of the Western cognoscenti hailed Buddhism as a kind of rational and humanistic psychology, Pallis' writings served as an implacable reminder of the Transcendent which is the fountainhead of all integral religious traditions and without which all the doings of mortals are nothing. He also exposed counterfeit forms of "Tibetan esoterism", such as the bizarre concoctions conjured up by "Lobsang Rampa" (one Cyril Hoskin). In explaining the Tibetan doctrines, some of them arcane and abstruse, Pallis was aided by the peerless metaphysical works of the great perennialists — René Guénon, Ananda Coomaraswamy and Frithjof Schuon. These enabled him to discern the universal significance of beliefs and practices which, at first glance, seemed strange and alien to untutored Western eyes. Also amongst Pallis' many achievements were fine translations of works by both Guénon and Schuon.

Pallis was not a prodigious writer. His essential *oeuvre* comprises three books: the present volume, first published in 1960, the more widely-known *Peaks and Lamas* (1939), and *A Buddhist Spectrum* (1980). *Peaks and Lamas*, recounting Pallis' early sojourns in Western Tibet and the Himalayan kingdoms, is a captivating work and one of the most distinguished works of the genre. *A Buddhist Spectrum* gathers together several essays from his later years, irradiated by a gentle but clear-eyed wisdom that was the fruit of his long years of study, spiritual practice and first-hand experience. In reviewing *A Buddhist Spectrum* Huston Smith remarked, "For insight, and the beauty insight requires if it is to be effective, I find no writer on Buddhism surpassing him".[1] This was high praise indeed from the doyen of contemporary comparative religionists, but amply justified. These are indeed works to cherish. But, assuredly, Pallis' master-work is *The Way and the Mountain*, focusing on the Tibetan tradition but situating it in the wider context of the perennial wisdom and the spiritual life which it entails. Pallis had no interest in research for its own sake, nor in any purely theoretical understanding of doctrine: his work was always attuned to the demands of the spiritual life itself. The essays to be found within these covers should be of interest not only to those on the Buddhist path but to all spiritual wayfarers.

There have been other Westerners whose writings are, to varying degrees, marked by acute metaphysical discernment, wide-ranging erudition, imaginative sympathy and a heartfelt love for Tibet and its people, but none have so pre-eminently combined these qualities as Pallis. One might mention not only Frithjof Schuon, whose few essays on Tibetan subjects are worth more than many shelves of orientalist studies, but figures such as Giuseppi Tucci, Lama Anagarika Govinda (formerly Ernst Hoffman), Hugh Richardson, David Snellgrove and Arnaud Desjardins. Nor should we forget the path-breaking labours of pioneers such as W.Y. Evans-Wentz and the redoubtable Alexandra David-Neel, or indeed of the first Tibetologists, those intrepid Jesuit scholars of the 17th and early 18th centuries. Then, too, there are the burgeoning works and teachings of the Tibetan diaspora, not least from the Dalai Lama himself, which keep alive at least some aspects of the tradition. But Marco Pallis, visiting Tibet at a fateful moment in its history and gifted with a rare metaphysical intelligence, had a singular role to play, testifying to the deepest significance of Tibet and its fate for the dark times in which we live. His works poignantly recall the beautiful and priceless treasures which have been so shamelessly destroyed. However, *The Way and the Mountain* is far more than an elegy; it is also an affirmation of that inviolable Spirit which cannot be destroyed.

FIVE EAST-WEST BRIDGE BUILDERS

SISTER NIVEDITA, RUDOLF OTTO, GIUSEPPE TUCCI, GARY SNYDER, HUSTON SMITH

...understanding, at least in realms as inherently noble as the great faiths of mankind, brings respect; and respect prepares the way for a higher power, love — the only power that can quench the flames of fear, suspicion, and prejudice, and provide the means by which the people of this small but precious Earth can become one to one another.

– Huston Smith[1]

A N ANGLO-IRISH disciple of Vivekananda, a German theologian, an Italian Tibetologist, an American Beat poet, and a scholar who wrote perhaps the century's most widely influential survey of the world's religions — these are the disparate figures, bound together by a fascination with the religious life of the East, to whom we now turn. We will combine biographical sketches with some general remarks about their significance as bridge-builders between the West and the East, and in so doing adumbrate several important themes and problematics.

SISTER NIVEDITA (MARGARET NOBLE)

> You will be in the midst of half-naked men and women with quaint ideas of caste and isolation, shunning the white skin through fear or hatred, and hated by them intensely. On the other hand, you will be looked upon by the whites as a crank, and every one of your moves will be watched with suspicion.[2]

So, in 1898, wrote an Indian swami to a young Anglo-Irish woman who had determined to follow him back to India as his disciple. He was the redoubtable Swami Vivekananda, by now probably the most widely known Indian in the Western world. She was Margaret Noble, thirty years old, daughter of a Congregationalist minister, journalist, headmistress of a progressive school in Wimbledon, agitator for Irish Home Rule, socialist champion of the poor, feminist and something of a firebrand. At Lady Ripon's Sesame Club she had met G.B. Shaw, Huxley and Yeats, and was well established in "a brilliant career" as writer, educationalist, lecturer and champion of "every kind of emancipation".[3]

Margaret Noble had earlier become disenchanted with the strict Protestant Christianity in which she was raised, and intellectually disturbed by the apparent conflict of religious faith and modern science, particularly Darwinism. For a time she was attracted to Buddhism but it was the Hindu tradition which was to become her spiritual refuge. Initially somewhat skeptical of the charismatic Bengali monk who was exciting such interest on his lecture tours of America and the United Kingdom, Noble found herself deeply attracted to the religious universalism which he had directly inherited from Ramakrishna, one of India's greatest saints and sages. Of Vivekananda's lectures she later wrote:

> The master's thought, which he continually approached from different points of view, [was] the equal truth of all religions, and the impossibility for us of criticizing any of the divine incarnations, since all were equally forth-shinings of the One.[4]

Another of Vivekanada's central themes also struck a chord: the primacy of spiritual experience over dogmas, creeds, sects, rites and institutions, and the ideal of realization as the supreme end of all religion.

Vivekananda was born Narendra Nath Datta[5] in Calcutta in 1863, into a wealthy family of scholars, philanthropists and monks.[6] At university Narendra had shown prodigious talents — intellectual, musical, theatrical, athletic — exhibiting all the vigour and vitality appropriate to the *Kshatriya* caste to which he belonged. He had an exceptionally intelligent, lively mind and an engaging personality, and seemed poised for a glittering career in law. Instead, answering an inner call which he had felt since childhood, Narendra turned his back on all worldly enticements and ambitions, and became one of the principal disciples of Ramakrishna at Dakshineswar, eventually becoming Swami Vivekananda.

Some years after the death of his master in 1886 Vivekananda attended the World's Parliament of Religions in Chicago and lectured extensively in America, the UK and Europe. An address to the graduate students in the philosophy department at Harvard generated such enthusiasm that he was forthwith offered a chair in Eastern Philosophy, an offer which his monastic vocation obliged him to decline.[7] His charismatic personality, his spiritual teachings and his nerve-tingling oratory generated a good deal of fervour and it was at this time that he attracted several Westerners who were to be amongst his most devoted and energetic disciples: from England, Captain Sevier and his wife, Josiah J. Goodwin who became the recorder of Vivekananda's lectures, and Margaret Noble. Vivekananda returned to India in a blaze of triumphant publicity and soon turned his considerable energies to the founding of the Ramakrishna Order, Mission and Math. In *Ramakrishna and His Disciples* Christopher Isherwood usefully summarized the aims of the Mission:

> The Mission will preach the truths which Ramakrishna preached and demonstrated in his own life. It will help others to put these truths into practice... It will train men to teach such knowledge or sciences as are conducive to the material and spiritual welfare of the masses. It will establish centers for monastic training and social work in different parts of India. It will also send trained members of the Order to countries outside India, to bring a better relation and a closer understanding between them. Its aims will be purely spiritual and humanitarian; therefore it will have no connection with politics.[8]

By the turn of the century Vivekananda had become closely, and somewhat reluctantly, associated with the cause of Indian nationalism as well as the burgeoning Hindu reform movement.

Margaret Noble arrived in Calcutta in January 1898. Thenceforth, until the early death of Vivekananda in 1902, aged forty, she was to be his closest Western disciple and was referred to by the monks of the order as his "spiritual daughter". Her biographer has described her initial reactions to a land so different from the Victorian drawing-rooms she had left behind:

> ...when, by [Vivekananda's] side she saw Calcutta for the first time — the teeming life of the city, the noise, the colour and the peaceful movements of the brown waters of the Ganges — she fell utterly and irrevocably in love — not with Calcutta, but with India. It was a love affair that hit her with immense force because it was so unexpected. She had wanted to help with the work, she had been eager to come, but she had not expected anything like this.[9]

She moved into a small cottage on the banks of the holy river with two of Vivekananda's other Western disciples, Josephine McCleod and Mrs. Ole Bull, widow of the Norwegian violinist and friend of Ibsen.

Noble took to heart Vivekananda's injunction:

> You have to set yourself to Hinduize your thoughts, your needs, your conceptions, and your habits. Your life, internal and external, has to become all that an orthodox Hindu Brahmin *Brahmacharini*'s ought to be.[10]

She succeeded remarkably well. She learnt Bengali, visited schools to understand the demands of her chosen field of work, underwent training with Vivekananda and took vows as a novice in the Ramakrishna order as Sister Nivedita ("the dedicated"). She overcame the initial suspicion, even hostility, of some of the monks of the Order and developed a close relationship with the Holy Mother, Sarada Devi (Ramakrishna's wife), with whom she lived for a time. She eventually moved into very humble quarters in one of Calcutta's poorest sectors where she established a school for girls, initially in her own house. (The school, much expanded, survives to this day as the Sister Nivedita School). Her lifestyle was frugal in the extreme. She also dedicated herself to working with the poor whom she served with indefatigable energy and was much admired by Indians for her heroic efforts during famine, flood and plague epidemics which afflicted Bengal around the turn of the century. She nurtured the education and social emancipation of Indian women, especially widows. Sister Nivedita also became a public speaker of some renown, lecturing on religious and social subjects. One of her early lectures, delivered in Calcutta's Albert Hall to a huge audience, was on the subject of Kali, the terrible goddess to whom Ramakrishna himself had been dedicated, and the controversial practice of Kali worship which she passionately defended against both Western and Indian detractors:

> We are aware [she said] of the many beastly and corrupt rites which have come to be associated with Kali worship. While our regret for them is boundless, we do not see the wisdom of inveighing against Kali-worship in wholesale manner... Destroy the weeds but save the garden![11]

This lecture, to be repeated in many parts of India, earned her acclaim in some quarters, notoriety in others. She later wrote what was to prove one of the most popular of her many books, *Kali the Mother* (much admired by Aurobindo). She accompanied Vivekananda on another tour of America and Britain and became a sought-after lecturer in her own right, using the proceeds to fund her school in Calcutta and her social work amongst the poor. She ignited a storm of controversy in London through her telling criticisms of the ways in which some Christian missionaries so persistently misrepresented Hinduism and the Indian social order. (She was scrupulous in avoiding any criticism of their religious teachings).[12]

By the time of Vivekananda's death she had left far behind her the naïve British patriotism with which she had arrived in the sub-continent and had become a champion of Indian independence and a fierce critic of the colonial regime, a role for which she was peculiarly well-equipped:

> Her entire nature fitted her for it; all the "fighting Irish" in her was awake; she had already proved that she could rouse large Hindu audiences to enthusiasm; she had the undoubted asset, in India, of being a disciple of their much-loved leader; she was a woman and a nun, and therefore a mother-figure and liable to be treated with respect; she was a member of the ruling nation by birth who had become totally a Hindu in thinking and loyalties... And she longed to fight for India...[13]

Because of the monastic prohibition on overt political activism she felt she must now sever her formal ties with the Ramakrishna Order but in her heart she remained true to her vows. She also continued her warm friendship with Sarada Devi, with the monks at the Math and with other Western devotees.

As a tireless critic of British rule and advocate of the nationalist cause she befriended such figures as Aurobindo Ghose, Rabindranath Tagore and various other members of that illustrious family, the Congressional leaders G.K. Gokhale and R.C. Dutt, and Mrs Annie Besant, leader of the Indian branch of the Theosophical Movement. She had a fleeting meeting with the young Gandhi, still a somewhat peripheral figure in the independence movement, who later wrote of her in the most respectful terms. In some respects she had anticipated some of the themes central to Gandhi's later campaigns. After meeting the Russian anarchist Prince Kropotkin in London, and reading his work, she had written:

> He knows more than any other man what India needs. What I specially dwell upon is the utter needlessness of governments...the village system supplies machinery of self-government enough...we shall one day peacefully wait upon the Viceroy and inform him, smiling, that his services are no longer required. The great means of doing it will be elaborated by degrees as we come to have what Mr Geddes calls "a theory of the Pacific Life".[14]

She spoke on political themes in many parts of India and published in a wide variety of newspapers and journals, for a time editing Aurobindo's *Karma Yogin*. Nivedita left her Calcutta school in the capable hands of her friend Sister Christine,[15] and in 1902, 1904, and again in 1907, spoke at venues all over the sub-continent on both religious and political subjects. She was an eloquent advocate for the *swadeshi* movement (the boycott of British-made goods) and an equally forceful opponent of Bengali partition, imposed by Curzon in 1905. As Gandhi was to do, she enjoined Muslims and Hindus to stand side-by-side as Indians:

> What then was the duty of the Indian Mussalman? It was not to relate himself to Arabia...he had no need of that; it had been accomplished for him by the faith and patient labour of his fore-fathers. No; his duty was to relate himself to India — his home by blood or by adoption and hospitality...[16]

Nor did she have any patience with one of the constant themes of imperialist propaganda — that "India" enjoyed no unity beyond that "given" to her by her benevolent colonizers:

> There is a religious idea that may be called Indian, but it is of no single sect;...there is a social idea, which is the property of no caste or group;...there is a historic evolution, in which we are all united;...it is the thing within all these which alone is called "India".[17]

Furthermore, she claimed, "the presence of a foreign bureaucracy adds immensely to the evil characteristics of the modern epoch".[18]

Her friend H.W. Nevinson has left us a vivid pen-portrait of Sister Nivedita at this time:

> It is as vain to describe Sister Nivedita in two pages as to reduce fire to a formula and call it knowledge...Like fire, and like Shiva, Kali and other Indian powers of the spirit, she was at once destructive and creative, terrible and beneficent. There was no dull tolerance about her, and I suppose no one ever called her gentle...[19]

In fact, she was capable of great sensitivity and gentleness, evident in her loving nursing of Gopaler-Ma, an elderly disciple of Ramakrishna who survived him by many years and for whom Nivedita always showed the most tender solicitude, as for Sarada Devi. But this was not the public face she exposed in pursuing the Indian cause.

Sister Nivedita published a good many books in her lifetime, some of the better-known being *Kali the Mother*, *The Web of Indian Life*, *Footfalls of Indian History*, *Cradle Tales of Hinduism* (for children) and her hagiography of Vivekananda, *The Master as I Saw Him*. Of these only the last retains much interest for the modern reader. Nonetheless, in their day they did much to dispel some of the prejudices and misconceptions about Hinduism and India which were rampant in the West, and helped to awaken in Indians a renewed sense of pride in their own religious and cultural heritage. In her later years she became deeply interested in traditional Indian art and a ferocious critic, in both the Indian and English press, of the then widely held "Hellenic theory" which postulated the Greek origins of Indian art — recall the episode in Kipling's *Kim* in the Lahore Museum where the lama "in open-mouthed wonder" beholds "the Greco-Buddhist sculptures done, savants know how long since, by forgotten workmen whose hands were feeling...for the mysteriously transmitted Grecian touch."[20] It was left to Nivedita's friend Ananda Coomaraswamy finally to demolish the Hellenic theory in 1927, after pointing out in the course of his argument that:

> ...this [Hellenic] view was put forward, as M. Fouchet [one of its principal exponents] himself admits, in a manner best calculated to flatter the prejudices of European students and to offend the susceptibilities of Indians: the creative genius of

Greece had provided a model which had later been barbarized and degraded by races devoid of true artistic instincts, to whom nothing deserving the name fine art could be credited.[21]

In the domain of the arts and crafts Sister Nivedita sought to reanimate traditional Indian ideals and in this campaign too she fought under the same banner as Coomaraswamy:

> ...we would remind all students of art that their true function
> is the revelation of the beautiful, the true, the good. It is not
> the fugitive moments of personal experience, but the eternal
> and universal, that best comes to the world through them.[22]

Her last years were marked by illness and the apparent defeat of her most cherished projects: the partition of Bengal had taken place; nationalist activities had been repressed and there was a hiatus in the independence movement, many of its leaders in prison, hiding or exile; her school was foundering; attempts to establish the Ramakrishna Mission in England had thus far met with meagre success. She was not to know that all these vicissitudes were temporary and that she had sown many seeds which were to germinate in the following decades. She would have been surprised to know that in 1967, on the centenary of her birth, an Indian stamp was issued in her honour. However, she seemed to have reached the inner quietitude of the authentic karma yogi, attaining that detachment from the fruits of one's work which is so exalted in the *Bhagavad Gita*. She died in Darjeeling in 1911 after contracting a fatal strain of dysentery. The epitaph on her tomb reads, "Here repose the ashes of Sister Nivedita, who gave her all for India."[23]

Rudolf Otto

In Europe 1917 marked a year of war, revolution, widespread dislocation, a mood of confusion, anxiety and nihilism. It was the year in which Rudolf Otto's book *Das heilege* appeared. It was to become one of the century's most influential books on the nature of religious experience, in some ways a descendant of William James' *The Varieties of Religious Experience* (1902). Soon translated into all the major European languages it was immensely popular in the decade after its publication. As Eric Sharpe wittily observed, it is a book that nearly every comparative religionist imagines they have read.[24]

The Idea of the Holy (its English title) was an attempt to establish a category under which religious experience could be understood in its own right, free of any theoretical schema imported from outside. It was also an attempt to valorize the non-rational (as distinct from the irrational) elements of religion. Otto's work was attuned to the spirit of Pascal's maxim:

> ...if one subjects everything to reason our religion will lose its mystery and its supernatural character. If one offends the principles of reason our religion will be absurd and ridiculous... These are two equally dangerous extremes, to shut reason out and to let nothing else in.[25]

In 1913 Otto's friend, the Swedish theologian Nathan Söderblom, had written, "Holiness is the great word in religion; it is even more essential than the notion of God".[26] Otto's purpose was to recuperate the full meaning of the word "holy" and to take hold of the religious experience to which this word points. Otto believed the word had become contaminated by moral associations which were quite secondary to its fundamental meaning and turned to an old Latin word *numen* to signal the realm of the most profound religious experience. The holy, he wrote, "is a category peculiar to religion.... [it] is perfectly *sui generis* and irreducible to any other; and therefore, like every absolutely primary and elementary datum, while it admits of being discussed, it cannot be defined"[27] but only evoked on the basis of experience. To experience the numinous is to encounter the *mysterium trememdum* which is marked by an overpowering sense of otherness, of awefulness, majesty and energy but which is also *fascinans* — beautiful, alluring, captivating. This real presence, neither a phantom nor a projection of the sub-conscious but, in Christian terms, the "living God", calls up "creaturely feeling" and appears "in a form ennobled beyond measure where the soul held speechless, trembles inwardly to the furthest fibre of its being".[28] In an Appendix Otto reproduces the thrilling passage from the *Bhagavad Gita* where Arjuna "smitten with amazement" beholds the manifold forms of Krishna, more dazzling than "the light of a thousand suns".[29]

Part of the book's appeal, for both general reader and for the student of religion, was Otto's understanding of religion primarily in experiential rather than credal terms. At a time when "religion" was often understood to hinge on belief and morality, Otto turned attention to the religious experience, not to offer any reductionistic "scientific" explanation but to affirm its mystery and power, and its centrality in religion. Comparative religionists were later to take up Otto's interest in the holy (now more often than not termed "the sacred") as one of the structuring principles of their inquiries. Unhappily, the very popularity of this germinative work has somewhat obscured Otto's many other achievements, not least in the field of Indological studies and in the promotion of global interreligious understanding.

Otto was born in 1869 in Northern Germany, into a strict Lutheran family, the twelfth of thirteen children.[30] He studied theology, languages, music and art at the universities of Erlangen and Gottingen. The young theologian was disenchanted with the "ossified intellectualism" of the prevailing rationalistic theology and was strongly attracted to Martin Luther's insistence that the knowledge of God had little to do with the rational faculties.[31] Indeed, Otto's dissertation for his licentiate in theology was on Luther's view of the Holy Spirit and he repeatedly returned to the Pauline maxim that "the letter killeth but the spirit giveth life." Otto was also much influenced in his early years by Kant, Schleiermacher, Fries, Albrecht Ritschl and Ernest Troeltsch, each of whom provided a strong antidote to the reigning theological orthodoxies of the period. Otto was swimming against the tide of the regnant theologians of the day, Rudolf Bultmann, Karl Barth and Emil Brunner, a tide which "overwhelmed Otto at the pinnacle of his career, and resulted in a widespread rejection of his work among theologians".[32] Nearly half a century later Karl Barth recalled this uncongenial climate:

> Everything that even from afar smelt of mysticism and morals, of pietism and romanticism or even idealism, how suspect it was and how strictly prohibited or confined in the straitjacket of restrictions.[33]

Otto trained for the Lutheran ministry and after two years in a theological seminary he traveled to the Middle East. In Cairo he was profoundly influenced by the Coptic liturgy, by some Jewish rites in Jerusalem and by a Dervish ceremony which he described as "unspeakable". After these experiences, formative in his intellectual and spiritual development, he returned to Germany via the great monastic center at Mt Athos where he spent ten days. This trip provided the catalyst for his great intellectual enterprise, the construction of "a methodology of religious feeling".

Otto was neither Indologist nor comparative religionist: his professional life, apart from brief stints in the Lutheran ministry and as a member of the Prussian Parliament, was as an academic systematic theologian. He was appointed to a position at Göttingen University in 1898 where he worked before moving as a full professor to Breslau in 1915, and three years later to Marburg where he succeeded the illustrious Wilhelm Herrmann. He wrote on a wide range of religious subjects and lectured at many universities on both sides of the Atlantic. Joachim Wach has left us a vivid pen portrait of Otto in his later years:

> Rudolf Otto was an imposing figure. He held himself straight and upright. His movements were measured. The sharply cut countenance kept a grave expression which did not change much even when jesting. The colour of his skin was yellowish-white and betrayed past illness. Otto had contracted a tropical disease in India which forced him ever after to husband his strength strictly. His hair was white and clipped...A small white moustache covered his upper lip. His most fascinating features were his steel-blue eyes. There was a rigidity in his glance, and one had the impression that he was "seeing" something, as he spoke, to which his interlocutor had no access...An air of genuine mystery surrounded Otto. Familiarity was the last thing which a visitor would have expected of the great scholar or he himself would have encouraged. The students who followed his lectures tensely and with awe called him the Saint...neither before nor since my meeting Otto have I known a person who impressed one more genuinely as a true

mystic. There was something about him of the solitude into which an intimate communion with the Divine has frequently led those who were favoured in this way.[34]

Nine of Otto's books appeared in English in the interwar years but many of his essays have only recently appeared in English, thanks largely to the enterprise of Gregory Alles. He was throughout his adult life engaged in a range of extra-academic activities — the movement for liturgical and ecclesiastical reform (including the creation of ministries for women), electoral change and efforts to establish an international Religious League. Ill health forced Otto's early retirement in 1929. He died of pneumonia in 1937, shortly after suffering an almost fatal sixty-foot fall from a tower which he had climbed in Staufenberg. The last years of his life were marred by severe illness, morphine addiction, depression and possibly more severe psychiatric disturbance; it is possible that Otto's "fall" was a suicide attempt.[35] The inscription on Otto's tomb in Marburg is "*Heilig, Heilig, Heilig, ist der Herr Zaboath*", the *sanctus* which had taken on a particular resonance in his life and work.

Otto's work falls quite neatly into two distinct periods: the early years of his professional life in which he was engrossed in teaching and writing about Protestant theology; and the later years in which his attention often turned Eastwards and towards more universal religious problems and themes. *The Idea of the Holy* is a kind of fulcrum between these two periods. In the present context it is Otto's engagement with the East which is our primary concern.

In 1911 Otto traveled extensively in North Africa, the Middle East and India: his experiences were to be decisive in the gestation of *The Idea of the Holy*. In a now-famous passage in a letter to a German church weekly he described the effect of hearing the Trisagion of Isaiah in the synagogue in Moroccan Mogador:

> It is Sabbath, and already in the dark and inconceivably grimy passage of the house we hear that sing-song of prayers and reading of scripture, that nasal half-singing half-speaking which Church and Mosque have taken over from the Synagogue. The sound is pleasant, one can soon distinguish modulations and cadences that follow one another at regular intervals, like Leitmotive. The ear tries to grasp individual words but it is scarcely possible...when suddenly out of the babel of voices, causing a thrill of fear, there it begins, unified, clear and unmistakable: *Kadosh Kadosh Kadosh Elohim Adonai Zebaoth Male'u hashamayim wahaarets kebodo!* (Holy, holy, holy, Lord of hosts, the heavens and the earth are full of thy glory). I have heard the *Sanctus Sanctus Sanctus* of the cardinals in St Peters, the *Swiat Swiat* Swiat in the Cathedral of the Kremlin and the Holy Holy Holy of the Patriarch in Jerusalem. In whatever language they resound, these most exalted words that have ever come from human lips always grip one in the depths of the soul, with a mighty shudder exciting and calling into play the mystery of the other world latent therein. And this more than anywhere else here in this modest place, where they resound in the same tongue in which Isaiah first received them and from the lips of the people whose first inheritance they were.[36]

The Asian leg of his journey also left an abiding impression on Otto. Soon after arriving in Karachi he was astonished when a newly-met young Hindu launched into an eloquent discourse on the philosophy of Kant. Otto sailed up the Indus river to

Lahore and thence to Calcutta and Orissa where he was lavishly entertained by a Maharajah in whom he found an attractive blend of European learning and Hindu piety. In India he had sympathetic encounters with Muslims, Sikhs, Hindus and Parsees. From India Otto traveled to Burma where he was much impressed by the vitality of Theravadin Buddhism. In Japan he visited universities, temples and monasteries and may have been the first Westerner to address a large gathering of Zen monks. He went on to China where he stayed for two months before returning to Europe through Siberia, accompanied by a collection of priceless religious artifacts which he deposited in the Museum of World Religions which he established in Marburg.

Despite poor health Otto returned to India in 1927. He was by now an accomplished Sanskritist, had translated several early Vedic texts and had published his most important contribution to Western understanding of the Hindu tradition, *Mysticism East and West*, in which he continued Schopenhauer's association of Vedantic metaphysics and Meister Eckhart's apophatic theology. Whilst not unaware of "manifold singularities", Otto found in the mystics of both East and West "an astonishing conformity in the deepest impulses of human spiritual experience", independent of "race, clime and age".[37] As Richard King has noted, Otto's enterprise is coloured by his apparent intention to rehabilitate Eckhart's standing within German Protestantism through the comparison with Shankara — an example of "the projection of Christian theological debates...onto an Indian canvas".[38] Nonetheless, Otto's work remains a pioneering work of remarkable acuity in the field of comparative mysticism.

A visit to Elephanta Island (near Bombay), like his earlier experiences in the Middle East, left a profound impression on him. His description (often cited):

One climbs halfway up the mountainside on magnificent stone steps until a wide gate opens on the right, in the volcanic rocks. This leads into one of the mightiest of early Indian rock temples. Heavy pillars hewn out of the rock support the roof. The eye slowly accustoms itself to the semi-darkness, gradually distinguishes awesome representations — carved into the wall — of the religious epics of India, until it reaches the imposing central recess. Here an image rises up out of the rock which I can only compare with the great representations of Christ in early Byzantine churches. It is a three-headed form, carved only as far as the breast, in threefold human size...Still and powerful the central head looks down, with both the others in profile. Over the image rests a perfect peace and majesty... Nowhere else have I found the secret of the transcendent world, the other world more grandly and perfectly expressed than in these three heads...To see this place were alone worth a journey to India, while from the spirit of religion which has lived here, one may experience more in a single hour of contemplation than from all the books.[39]

After this second trip to India Otto wrote a good many scholarly works on the Vaisnavite tradition, translated several texts, including those of Ramanuja, the *Katha Upanishad* and the *Bhagavad Gita* with which he originally felt little sympathy but on which he was to write with considerable discernment.[40] Otto also wrote another comparison of his own tradition and Hinduism, *India's Religion of Grace and Christianity* (1928). Amongst his most interesting and penetrating essays was one on Gandhi whom Otto recognized as a distinctly Indian type. He also discerned in Gandhi the beneficent influence of the various religions to which he had been exposed and to whose ethical teachings he was peculiarly receptive — Jainism, Islam and Christianity, as well as his own Vaishnavite tradition.[41]

Although Otto was most strongly attracted to Hinduism, especially its medieval expressions, he also wrote sympathetically about Buddhism of both the Theravadin and Mahayana traditions and a percipient essay (1924) on Zen Buddhism at a time when it was virtually unknown in the West. Unlike many of his predecessors and contemporaries he did not find Buddhism either "nihilistic" or "pessimistic" and in Zen discerned a radical mystical method, "almost torn away from all rational schemata", aimed at a direct encounter with the numinous, the "wholly other".[42] In 1925 Otto wrote the preface to the first book on Zen in German, a collection of classical texts translated by Ohasama Shuei, entitled *Zen: Living Buddhism in Japan*. His later essay "Numinous Experience in Zen" has also been heralded as an important work.[43]

As early as 1913 Otto had conceived the idea of a *Religiöser Menschheitbund* (Interreligious League) which would bring together representatives of all the world's religions to work towards international peace, social justice and moral progress. In the sorry aftermath of World War I Otto pleaded eloquently and passionately for the RMB:

> I hope that the misery which all nations suffer today will finally teach them what religion and ethics should have taught them a long time ago: that they do not walk alone. People of every land and nation must constantly bear in mind that they face great collective tasks, and that to accomplish these tasks they need brotherly collaboration and cooperation. By themselves, political associations cannot do what is needed... Will [the League of Nations] become anything more than a "limited liability corporation" that

actively pursues the special interests of whatever groups temporarily find themselves in power...In and of themselves, institutions, laws, decrees, and negotiations are powerless. They require the continual support of an awakened collective conscience...

After commending the efforts of his friend, Swedish Archbishop Nathan Söderblom, to initiate a more lively and fertile Christian ecumenism (eventually leading to the formation of the World Council of Churches in 1948), Otto went on:

But Christianity hardly encompasses all of humanity...What would it mean if perhaps every three years those who represent the consciences of individual nations — the most influential leaders and emissaries of all churches all over the world — assembled publicly to discuss issues of universal concern, to display personally their common feeling for all of humanity, and then to take home a heightened will to create a global community? In time this assembly would develop into a forum that would be completely independent of the struggles and limitations of diplomacy. It could discuss the great issues of the day.

Otto's identification of those problems strikes a very contemporary note:

...issues of public and international morality, social and cultural issues that all nations share, unavoidable clashes between different nations and how to alleviate them, issues of class, gender, and race...The same body would also provide a natural court of appeals for oppressed minorities, classes, and nations.[44]

Under Otto's leadership the RMB actually flourished for a time in the 1920s and attracted participants from Asia and North America as well as many European countries. Otto's trip to the subcontinent in 1928-29 was principally to gain support for the RMB, efforts which met with considerable success. It was dissolved in 1933 but was revived by Friedrich Heiler and Karl Küssner in 1956 and thereafter became the German branch of the World Congress of Faiths which had been founded early in the century by Sir Francis Younghusband.

Although Otto's work has been strangely neglected in the Western world over the last fifty years there is no doubting his influence on both theologians and comparative religionists. For many years Paul Tillich alone amongst German theologians really carried Otto's banner but the climate today, in which "theologians now inhabit a world of religious pluralism, uncertain truth claims, and interreligious dialogue" may well make Otto's ideas congenial once again.[45] Amongst comparative religionists his legacy was perhaps most evident in the work of his compatriot Joachim Wach but Otto also palpably influenced figures such as Mircea Eliade, Friedrich Heiler, Gerardus van der Leeuw and Ugo Bianchi. As early as 1912 he had struck a prophetic note with these words:

> We in the West now realize that we have no monopoly of religious truth. We must in honesty change our attitude towards other faiths, for our watchword must be "Loyalty to truth". This changed attitude, however, does not weaken, but

rather, instead, reinforces one's faith in God, for He is seen to be not a small or partial being but the Great God who is working throughout all times and places and faiths.[46]

The ideals for which Otto strived and the values he upheld, both within the Church and in the wider world, have lost none of their pertinence or urgency.

GIUSEPPE TUCCI

Shortly after the death of Giuseppe Tucci, in 1984, Mircea Eliade wrote of the Italian Tibetologist:

> Giuseppe Tucci was one of those rare scholars whose biographies cannot be reduced to their bibliographies. His learning was vast and profound, his linguistic and historiographical erudition reminds us of such giants as Paul Pelliot or Berthold Laufer, and his writings (some sixty volumes and more than two hundred articles) are of an amazing variety of contents and literary styles. But Giuseppe Tucci was also a prodigious traveler and an indefatigable explorer.[47]

Unlike many contemporaneous Tibetologists, Tucci actually made extended visits to Tibet: between 1927 and 1948 he visited Tibet and the contiguous Himalayan kingdoms no less than eight times. Edward Conze tells us that Tucci believed that the friendly reception he was accorded in Tibet derived from the fact that in a previous life he had been a Tibetan who decided to be reborn in the West in order to help his people.[48] He had earlier spent five years in India (1925-30), and later, in the 50s, directed two expeditions to Nepal.[49] He combined in himself the qualities of the explorer, naturalist, linguist and scholar. Tucci was one of the last links in a very long chain of Italian exploration of the Tibeto-Himalayan region, stretching back to Marco Polo and running through such figures as the Jesuit missionary and scholar Father Ippolito Desideri and the celebrated mountaineer, the Duke of Abruzzi. In *Tibet, Land of Snows* (1967) Tucci describes his impressions of both the landscape and the culture in rhapsodic prose:

> Only those who have been in Tibet know the fascination of its huge landscapes, its diaphanous air that scarfs the icy peaks with turquoise, its vast silence that at once humbles man and uplifts him.[50]

Elsewhere we find him writing this:

> In Tibet, a land I know well and have often visited, I have always dwelt under the impression that I found myself in a place not only remote in space, but above all remote in time, as if by betaking myself there, I had by a work of magic gone backwards in the path of centuries, or evoked...a society, such as it would have been around the year one thousand of our era: the same intenseness of spiritual life, the same religious bent, the same want of distinctness, even lack of boundaries between reality and imagination...[51]

The trope of Tibet as "medieval survival", a "timeless reliquary", was a popular one in many European writings of the time and was given perhaps its most extended and poignant expression in

Secret Tibet (1952), by Fosco Mariani, Tucci's photographer on his last Tibetan expedition.[52]

Tucci recounted his experiences on the 1948 expedition in *To Lhasa and Beyond*. He visited Western Tibet and joined pilgrimages to Mt Kailas and Lake Manasarovar. "Those places", he wrote, "deserve to be sacred, if for nothing else, for the natural beauty God lavished on them in the luckiest days of His creation".[53] He also visited Tibet's ancient Western capital, Sakya, where he explored its temples and libraries while the 1948 expedition included researches in Shigatse, Gyantse and the Yarlung Valley as well as Lhasa and the great monasteries of Drepung, Sera and Ganden. He was accompanied on part of this expedition by Sherpa Tenzing, soon to ascend Mt Everest with Edmund Hilary.[54] Tenzing recalls his meeting with Tucci:

> Professor Tucci was a strange man: indeed, one of the most remarkable I have ever met. He was very serious and absolutely devoted to his work. But, unlike the mountaineers I had known, who were mostly quiet men, he was terrifically excitable and temperamental, and everything had to be just so, or there was a great explosion...But in time I grew to like Professor Tucci as well as any man I have ever known...he was a great scholar, knowing much more about the country than the people who lived there. And I have never been able to count how many languages he knew. Often his conversations to me would begin in one, change suddenly to another, and end up in a third...From him I learned all sorts of things.[55]

To Lhasa and Beyond includes a fascinating account of Tucci's highly formal audience with the fourteen-year old Dalai Lama who, more than three decades later, was warmly to commend a new edition of the book, writing, "Tucci's description of the timeless civilization of the Tibetan people is as perceptive and relevant today as it was when he wrote the book thirty years ago".[56]

Tucci was born in 1894 in Macerata (Adriatic Italy), the birthplace of the 18th century Capuchin Tibetologist, Cassiano Beligatti. His intellectual development was precocious and he rapidly mastered Greek and Latin, his first published article being on some Latin inscriptions found near his home town. He graduated from the University of Rome and turned firstly to Chinese subjects, translating Mencius and producing a history of early Chinese philosophy. By the mid-20s his interests were concentrated on India, in particular Mahayana Buddhism. Tucci spent five fertile years in India, lecturing at the universities of Shantiniketan and Calcutta, developing many friendships with Indian pandits and writers, including Rabindranath Tagore, and laying the foundations for "a series of accurate and philologically impeccable" editions of Mahayana texts.[57] It was also in Calcutta that Tucci first met Mircea Eliade with whom he was to have a long association.[58] Soon after his return to Italy he was appointed to the Chair of Chinese at the Oriental Institute in Naples before moving on to the University of Rome as Professor of Religions and Philosophies of India and the Far East. Tucci remained in this position until his retirement in 1969. Tucci's scholarly work was by no means restricted to the realm of Tibetan Buddhism. Indeed, by the time he turned to Tibetan studies, in the early 30s, he was already an authority on a staggeringly diverse range of Oriental subjects. A recent bibliography of Tucci's work, probably incomplete, runs to some 360 items.[59]

The Tibetan phase of Tucci's career lasted from the early 30s until about 1950 by which time the Chinese invasion had put a stop to the field trips which Tucci had undertaken so often in the previous two decades. Nonetheless, Tibet had left a deep spiritual imprint on him: he kept a shrine in his home and regarded himself as a practitioner of the Kagyu school.[60] In his later years Tucci carried out archaeological work in Nepal, in the region of the Afghani-Pakistan border, and in Iran, also writing extensively on related subjects. During the 30s Tucci founded the Italian Institute for the Middle and Far East (IsMEO), a center for research and cultural exchanges, and the publisher of two important periodicals, *Asiatica* and *East and West*. It was largely through his role at IsMEO that Tucci became entangled in fascist politics. Gustavo Benavides has examined the linkages between Tucci's ideological leanings — overtly fascist in the pre-world War II period — and his representation of "the East", particularly Tibet. The collusion of Orientalism and fascism is an important but hazardous territory into which we will venture only later in this study. Here we are concerned principally with Tucci's contribution to 20th century Tibetology.

Tucci was always warmly welcomed in Tibet where he impressed his hosts by his ability to engage in lively philosophical disputations with Tibetan lamas in their own language. They were often astonished to discover that Tucci knew more about the texts and sacred objects in the many monasteries that he visited than did their custodians.[61] His expertise in the *Vajrayāna* extended through Tantra, iconography, philosophy and metaphysics, folk music, and the study of royal tombs. Much of his scholarly work from this period is found in the massive seven-volume series *Indo-Tibetica* (1932-1941). His Tibetan masterwork was *Tibetan Painted Scrolls* (1959) — "a real *summa* of the art, literature, religion and history of Tibet"[62] and "a prodigious, learned and original contribution" to the study of *Vajrayāna*.[63] (So lavishly produced is this volume that it is infrequently seen outside the rare book collections of a few select universities).[64] The bent of Tucci's most significant work was archaeological, historical and philological rather than comparative and phenomenological. He also produced travel books and widely-read works of a more popular nature, including *The Theory and Practice of the Mandala* (1949) and *The Religions of Tibet* (1970), and produced an important Italian translation of *The Tibetan Book of the Dead* (1949). In his monograph on the mandala, at that time still only sketchily understood in the West, Tucci alludes positively to the pioneering work of Carl Jung in this field, but then goes on to articulate a principle which was to become one of the cornerstones of the so-called phenomenological method of comparative religious studies:

> My desire has been to discuss the mandala in such a way that I shall not misrepresent the opinions of the Indian Masters. In other words, I have been at pains not to lend to the ideas they express anything which might render those ideas incomprehensible to the men who formulated them.[65]

Tucci's critics, particularly those anatomizing some of the ideological fault lines in European Orientalism, have made much of the oppositions (eg. the historical, time-burdened, "progressive" West vs. the "mystical" and "timeless" East) which are doubtless to be found in his work. Nonetheless, in this context, it is interesting to come across a passage such as the following, written in 1958. Of the East-West divide, an ever-present theme in the Orientalist literature, Tucci had this to say:

> There is again much talk of the means of attaining a better reciprocal understanding between East and West. Having

stated the problem in this way, it is plain to everyone that an antithesis is implicitly involved...between Asia on one side, and Europe and its American extension on the other...but... Europe and Asia have since the dawn of history been closely joined and intercommunicating through migrations, invasions, conquests, trade, pilgrimages and interchanges of the arts and ideas, so that not one single event of any significance has ever occurred in one part without its [reaction] on the other, thus establishing the just claim to a common history, a history, that is, of the Euro-Asian continent. At any rate, to revert to our argument, men of culture who, if they be really so, have always been messengers of spiritual understanding, have never believed in any such differences between East and West.[66]

GARY SNYDER

In his autobiography Alan Watts describes Gary Snyder as:

a wiry sage with high cheek-bones, twinkling eyes, and a thin beard, and the recipe for his character requires a mixture of Oregon woodsman, seaman, Amerindian shaman, oriental scholar, San Francisco hippie, and swinging monk, who takes tough discipline with a light heart.[67]

Jack Kerouac had already conferred a kind of immortality on Snyder through the character of Japhy Ryder in *The Dharma Bums*. Snyder, born in California in 1930, was raised on small farms in Washington and Oregon. As a young man he worked as logger, seaman, fire-look-out and trail crew worker for the US Forest Service. Snyder had been interested in Asian cultures since being impressed as a boy by Chinese landscape paintings in the Seattle

Art Museum. At Reed College Snyder studied anthropology, linguistics, literature and American Indian culture. While still a student, and with his friend Philip Whalen, Snyder began a systematic and disciplined study of Buddhism after reading translations of the Chinese classics by Pound and Waley in the late 40s, and R.H. Blyth's four-volume translation, *Haiku* (1949-1952) — also being read by his friends Kenneth Rexroth, Jack Kerouac and Allen Ginsberg.[68] In 1951 D.T. Suzuki's *Essays in Zen Buddhism* provided Snyder's first introduction to Zen, and helped him to understand some of the connections between Hinduism, Buddhism and Taoism. Snyder also developed an abiding interest in Chinese and Japanese poetry, and undertook translations of works such as the poems of Han Shan ("Cold Mountain"). In an interview in the mid-50s he characterized the Beat movement this way:

> In a way the Beat Generation is a gathering together of all the available models and myths of freedom in America that had existed before, namely: Whitman, John Muir, Thoreau, and the American bum. We put them together and opened them out again, and it becomes a literary motif, and then we added some Buddhism to it.[69]

His interest in Buddhism ran so deep that in May 1956, aided by Alan Watts and Ruth Fuller Sasaki, he left America to spend much of the next ten years in study in Japan, becoming a disciple of Rinzai Zen master Oda Sesso Roshi, Abbot of Daitoku-ji in Kyoto, and eventually taking lay monastic vows.[70] (Snyder is but one of a wave of westerners who have found their way into Japanese monasteries since Rudolf Otto's visit in 1912: in the last five decades one may mention such figures as Ruth Fuller

Sasazki, Philip Kapleau, Robert Aitken, Irmgard Schloegl, Jan van der Wetering, Harold Stewart, Clive Faust, Karlfried Graf Dürckheim, Elsie Mitchell, Richard Baker, Jiyu Kennett, Gerta Ital, Peter Matthiessen). Snyder returned briefly to America in 1958 and was one of the contributors to a special "Zen" issue of the *Chicago Review*, a signpost to the mushrooming American interest in Zen. The issue included Snyder's essay "Spring Sesshin at Sokoku-ji", Alan Watts' "Beat Zen, Square Zen, and Zen", translations of Chinese and Japanese spiritual classics by D.T. Suzuki and Ruth Fuller Sasaki, poems by Kerouac and Whalen.[71] Snyder also traveled throughout India in 1962 with Joanne Kyger and Allen Ginsberg, recounting experiences which "deepened, widened and saddened" his mind in *Passage through India*.[72] They visited Bodhgaya and the Deer Park of Sarnath and had an audience with the Dalai Lama: the main subject of their questionings seems to have been drug-induced experiences (one of the staples of both the Beat and hippie movements in which Snyder and Ginsberg were leading lights).[73] In a more recent Foreword to that book Snyder highlights his understanding of India this way:

I honor India for many things: those neolithic cattle breeders who sang daily love songs to God and Cow, as a family, and whose singing is echoed even today in the recitation of the Vedas and the sutra chanting of Los Angeles and Japan. The finest love poetry and love sculpture on earth. Exhaustive meditations on mind and evocations of all the archetypes and images. Peerless music and dance. But most, the spectacle of a high civilization and accomplished art, literature and ceremony without imposing a narrow version of itself on every tribe and village. Civilization without centralization or monoculture... no culture but India prior to modern times imagined such a scale of being — light years vast universes, light year size leaps of time. Dramas of millions of lifetimes reborn. How did they do it? Soma? Visitors from Outer Space? Nah. I think just Big Mind drank in with Himalayan snow-melt rivers and seeing Elephant's ponderous daintiness, and keeping ancient shamanistic sages and forest hermits fed on scraps of food, to hear and respect their solid yoga studies. The Buddha Shakyamuni, one of those, was loved, and listened to by cowgirls, traders, and courtesans.[74]

After his return from Japan Snyder plunged into the late 60s counter-culture which was "eclectic, visionary, polytheistic, ecstatic and defiantly devotional".[75] More distinctively, he "attempted to work out an alternative ethic which drew on both Buddhist and native American ideals, as well as American natural rights ideology",[76] an ethic which he expressed in his poetry, his talks and essays (which reveal considerable though lightly-worn learning and a mind of great suppleness), and through social and ecological activism. His capsule summary of Buddhist teachings: "impermanence, no-self, the inevitability of suffering and connectedness, emptiness, the vastness of mind, and a way to realization".[77] Taking his cue from Blake's "Energy is Eternal Delight", in *Turtle Island* Snyder wrote this:

Delight is the innocent joy arising
with the perception and realization of
the wonderful, empty, intricate,
inter-penetrating,
mutually-embracing, shining
single world beyond all discriminations

or opposites.

In a nutshell, Buddhist metaphysic as the basis for ecological awareness. Throughout his life Snyder has been deeply concerned with "our ethical obligations to the nonhuman world", a notion, he says, which "rattles the foundations of occidental thought".[78] Thanks to the sustained efforts of poets and writers like Snyder, Wendell Berry, and Wes Jackson (amongst many others) the idea now has a much wider currency. Also among Snyder's most notable achievements has been his sensitive and intelligent receptivity to the traditions of the American Indians.[79]

Snyder has also been one of a stream of writers who have drawn on Eastern spirituality and philosophy in their attempts to fashion a new aesthetic and fresh expressive modes — poetic, in Snyder's case. As one commentator noted:

> All of Snyder's study and work has been directed toward a poetry that would approach phenomena with a disciplined clarity and that would then use the "archaic" and "primitive" as models to once again see this poetry as woven through all parts of our lives.[80]

Snyder has published several collections of essays and some fifteen-odd volumes of poetry, one of which, *Turtle Island* (1974) was awarded the Pulitzer Prize. A useful compendium of four decades of essays on culture, nature and poetics is *A Place in Space: Ethics, Aesthetics, and Watersheds* (1996). He has often been interviewed in the organs of counter-cultural America, has pounded the "alternative" lecture circuit visiting, he says, "practically every university in the United States"[81] and has been an energetic advocate of many progressive and ecological causes — the "unofficial poet laureate of the environmentalist movement". Along with Robert Aitken, Joanna Macy, and Richard Baker he was a founder, in 1978, of the Buddhist Peace Fellowship, a sign of the increasing interest amongst Western dharma practitioners in welding together Eastern spiritual practice and Western forms of social and political activism; "engaged Buddhism" became one of the labels by which such concerns came to be identified. This vein of "spiritual politics" has many antecedents in American Romanticism and Transcendentalism; as someone recently remarked, "If Ginsberg is the Beat movement's Walt Whitman, Gary Snyder is the Henry David Thoreau".[82] In recent years Snyder has evinced more interest in a non-adversarial political agenda, has become more open to bhaktic forms of religious practice, and has been increasingly influenced by the great 13th century master Dogen Zenji.[83] He still practices *zazen* ("sitting meditation"). Let us leave Snyder with the words of Jim Dodge:

> Having achieved the "mythopoetic interface of society, ecology, and language" that he chose as his fields of inquiry, his point of multiple attention, Gary Snyder is justly honored as an elder in the environmental movement, a revolutionary social critic, an excellent translator, a Buddhist scholar and eminent practitioner, and, of course, a premier poet. He is also a nature writer of surpassing lucidity...one of the great synthesizing intellects of our age...[and] a Warrior of the Imagination...[84]

HUSTON SMITH

If Otto's *The Idea of the Holy* was one of the most widely read books on religion of the inter-war period, Huston Smith's *The Religions of Man* must surely be the most popular of the second half of the century. First published in 1958 it has been in print ever since, selling millions of copies and now re-titled as *The World's Religions: Our Great Wisdom Traditions*.[85] The hallmarks of Smith's approach to the comparative study of the world's religions were evident from the outset: the conviction that each religious tradition was the repository of timeless truths and values; the attempt to understand the forms and practices of any particular tradition from the viewpoint of its adherents; an intuitive sympathy which enabled Smith to "tune into" a wide diversity of spiritual modalities; an understanding that the hyper-rationalism of much modern philosophy and the pseudo-scientific methodologies of the so-called social sciences were inadequate tools with which to grasp human realities; a style of exposition free of the specialized jargon of the disciplines on which Smith drew (most notably philosophy, theology, comparative religion) and one immediately accessible to the intelligent general reader. One might say that Smith's mode turned on a kind of natural courtesy and respect for the traditions he was exploring. He also situated the study of religion within an existential context:

> Religion alive confronts the individual with the most momentous option this world can present. It calls the soul to the highest adventure it can undertake, a proposed journey across the jungles, peaks and deserts of the human spirit. The call is to confront reality, to master the self. Those who dare to hear and follow this secret call soon learn the dangers and difficulties of its lonely journey.[86]

Since 1958 Smith's understanding of both the inner unity and the formal diversity of the world's integral religious traditions has been both deepened and sharpened by his encounter with the traditionalist perspective. Within the academic world he has been a passionate and eloquent spokesman for the traditionalist school, and has engaged many of the deepest problems and issues arising out of the contemporary collision of the forces of tradition and modernity. His essential vocation has been as an educator.

Smith was born in 1919 in Soochow, China.[87] His parents were missionaries and he was to spend the first seventeen years of his life in China. One of his former students, Philip Novak, writes:

> If you would know Huston Smith, start with China... Beholding him, one wonders whether fantastic tales about Chinese magic are not true after all. There is something distantly — and yet distinctly — Asian in his physiognomy. China paused on his skin, it seemed, before proceeding to his marrow...Open the pages of the *Analects* to Confucius's description of the *chun-tzu* (ideal gentleman) and you touch Huston's fiber. *Chun-tzu*...one who possesses a truly human heart, who cherishes the arts of learning and teaching, and who is as concerned to teach by moral example as by intellectual knack.[88]

After his schooling at the Shanghai American School Smith studied at the Central Methodist College in Fayette, Missouri, where his intellectual engagements were primarily theological and philosophical. Thereafter he pursued further studies at the prestigious Divinity School at the University of Chicago and at the University of California at Berkeley during which time, partly under the influence of the "Californian Vedantins" (Gerald Heard and Aldous Huxley amongst them) he became more deeply engaged in the study of mysticism. A series of teaching appointments followed at the universities of Denver and Colorado, Washington University in St Louis, the Massachusetts Institute of Technology (1958-1973) and Syracuse University (1973-1983). Early in his career Smith also served as a chaplain and associate minister in the Methodist Church, improbably combining these duties with the presidency of the St Louis Vedanta Society! In later years Smith has been one of the prime movers in the establishment of the Foundation of Traditional Studies, based in Washington D.C. and of which he is the Vice-President.[89] As the editor of a *festschrift* in his honour remarked:

> Professor Smith's teaching career has been devoted to bridging intellectual gulfs: between East and West, between science and the humanities, and between the formal education of the classroom and informal education via films and television.[90]

His films and television programs have focused on Hinduism, Buddhism, Sufism and Tibetan music. In 1996 Bill Moyers hosted a five-part PBS television series, *The Wisdom of Faith with Huston Smith*.

From Smith's wide-ranging scholarly *oeuvre* we may select three works of signal importance: *The Religions of Man*, a masterly and engaging conspectus of the world's major religious traditions; *Forgotten Truth: the Primordial Tradition* (1977) in which he expounds the perennial wisdom which lies at the heart of manifold sapiential doctrines and religious forms; and *Beyond the Post-Modern Mind* (1982) which elaborates a critique of the intellectual habits and prejudices of the prevailing contemporary worldview, particularly as it finds expression in the Western academic ethos and in the highly reductive disciplinary specializations which purport to "explain" religious phenomena. As well as these three major landmarks we should note a recent anthology of some of Smith's most important articles, *Essays on World Religion* (1992) which includes many pieces on Asian subjects — a sample of titles indicates the range of Smith's interests: "Transcendence in Traditional China", "Tao Now: An Ecological Statement", "A Note on Shinto", "Spiritual Discipline in Zen", "India and the Infinite", "Vedic Religion and the Soma Experience", "The Importance of the Buddha", "Tibetan Chant: Inducing the Spirit".

The most decisive shift in Smith's outlook occurred as a consequence of reading the works of Frithjof Schuon, the master expositor of the *religio perennis* in modern times. Smith had been introduced to the works of Guénon, Schuon and other traditionalists by Seyyed Hossein Nasr during his time at MIT. Smith:

> I discovered that [Schuon] situated the world's religious traditions in a framework that enabled me to honor their significant differences unreservedly while at the same time seeing them as expressions of a truth, that because it was single, I could affirm. In a single stroke I was handed a way of honoring the world's diversity without falling prey to relativism, a resolution I had been seeking for more than thirty years.[91]

One of the penalties of fame is the exposure to endless invitations to write Prefaces, Forewords, Introductions and the like. It is a measure of both his international standing and his generosity of spirit to note some of the books which Smith has helped introduce to a wider audience, many of which have become classics of their kind: Philip Kapleau's *The Three Pillars of Zen* (1967), Dwight Godard's *A Buddhist Bible* (1970), *Zen Mind, Beginner's Mind* (1970) by Shunryu Suzuki, S.H. Nasr's *Ideals and Realities of Islam* (1972), Frithjof Schuon's *The Transcendent Unity of Religions* (1975), Swami Prabhavananda's *The Spiritual Heritage of India* (1979), *On Having No Head* (1986) by D.E. Harding, *A Treasury of Traditional Wisdom* (1986) edited by Whitall Perry, W.T. Stace's *Mysticism and Philosophy* (1987), *The Wheel of Life* (1988) by John Blofeld, a new edition of *The Way of a Pilgrim* and *The Pilgrim Continues His Way* (1991).[92]

Whilst the Judeo-Christian tradition in which he was raised has provided Smith with a firm spiritual anchorage, his life and work alike testify to his willingness to immerse himself in the religious forms and practices of other traditions, not by way of any kind of syncretism or "universal" religion, but in the search for understanding and for "the light that is of neither East nor West".[93] Religious experience has been a watchword in his writings and amongst his own spiritual encounters we may note his boyhood exposure to a Confucian master, his spell as a Methodist minister, weekly sessions with a Vedantin swami, the practice of yoga and an intensive reading of the *Upanishads* and other Hindu Scriptures in the 1950s, a summer of meditation and koan-training in a Myoshinji monastery in Kyoto in the 60s (where he developed a close friendship with D.T. Suzuki, doyen of modern Zen scholars, and practiced Zen with dharma-brother Gary Snyder), his inquiries into the possible links between drug-induced experiences and mysticism, and his close association with traditionalist Sufis in Iran and the USA. He has been a sympathetic and no doubt exemplary guest in many Houses of the Spirit. As well as moving freely through the corridors of academia (where, it must be said, his ideas encountered some suspicion and skepticism as well as acclaim) he has met countless rabbis, clerics, swamis, Zen masters, lamas, mystics and the like; by all reports such meetings are marked by that rapport which arises out of the spontaneous and mutual recognition of the radiant spiritual maturity which marks those who have traveled a good distance on the path.

In the conclusion to the most recent edition of *The World's Religions* the author observes that we have just survived "the bloodiest of centuries; but if its ordeals are to be birth pangs rather than death throes, the century's scientific advances must be matched by comparable advances in human relations". Such advances depend on our ability to listen to voices from all over the planet and to nurture a peace:

> built not on ecclesiastical or political hegemonies but on understanding and mutual concern. For understanding, at least in realms as inherently noble as the great faiths of mankind, brings respect; and respect prepares the way for a higher power, love — the only power that can quench the flames of fear, suspicion, and prejudice, and provide the means by which the people of this small but precious Earth can become one to one another.[94]

Huston Smith: scholar, minister, teacher, culture critic, pilgrim, bridge-builder; in each of these roles he has served the cause of interreligious understanding with great distinction and, in the words of one of his students, with "honesty of person, penetrating sensitivity...and flowing kindness".[95]

NOTES ON "SPIRITUALITY"

*Outside tradition there can assuredly be found some relative truths...
but outside tradition there does not exist a doctrine that catalyzes
absolute truth and transmits liberating notions concerning total reality.*

– Frithjof Schuon[1]

" SPIRITUALITY" HAS become a rather fashionable catch-word, recently appropriated by all manner of people, many of whom are disillusioned with the sterile paradigms of the mechanistic, hyper-rationalistic, materialistic and utilitarian worldview which characterizes modernity but who are also often hostile to traditional religious forms which might provide the necessary antidotes. "Spirituality" stands as a banner under which some of the richness and complexity of human consciousness and experience can be rescued from various physiological and psychological reductionisms. While one might well sympathize with these efforts to combat what William Blake called the "Single Vision" of scientism it must be said at the outset that much of the present-day discussion of "spirituality" really amounts to a kind of sentimental indulgence in which the word itself can be made to mean almost anything — more often than not referring to some kind of vaguely-defined inner life or experience. If the term is to be at all useful we must establish a provisional definition of "spirituality" and make a few remarks about its relation to religion, outside of which the whole notion makes little sense.

"Spirituality" might be conceptualized in many ways. Here is one: spirituality is both *a mode of understanding* Reality, one in which we recognize the Spirit within us, "the immortal spark of God's Being, eternally living in the depths of man's soul",[2] and *a mode of being* wherein we conform ourselves to that Reality. Further, one might say that spirituality is the domain of human experience in which a transmutation of the soul leads, depending on the vocabulary at hand, to God, to the Self, to Nirvana. A Hindu swami asked to sum up the message of Hinduism replied this way: "God Is; God can be realized; to realize God is the supreme end of human life; God can be realized in many ways."

Whilst this kind of formulation poses problems for some religious perspectives it might here stand as a signpost to the spiritual life in general.

Implicit in the idea that spirituality concerns both understanding and being are the parallel notions of a doctrine (an account of Reality in both its absolute and relative "dimensions") and a path (a spiritual method, provided by religious forms, whereby one might live in accordance with the Will of Heaven). One of the myriad problems surrounding many contemporary attitudes to "spirituality" is that the doctrine of an Ultimate Reality (by whatever name — the Absolute, God, Allah, Atman, Brahman, Nirvana/*Shūnyatā*, the Tao, *Wakan-Tanka*) and the elaboration of a spiritual method attuned to our relationship therewith, are left out of the picture altogether! What we are offered instead is a notion of "spirituality" as some kind of subjective inner state, a kind of "warm fuzzy glow", sometimes harnessed to formulations such as "the kingdom of Heaven is within you" — as if by these words Christ meant that the kingdom of Heaven is of a psychological order! This is all of a piece with the notion that "spirituality" is a private affair, and that the spiritual life can be fashioned out of the subjective resources of the individual in question. Some of the factors which, over several centuries, have conspired to create a climate in which such ideas could take root include the rebellion against all authority, the cult of the individual, the humanistic prejudice that "man is the measure of all things", the triumph — even in the religious domain itself — of sentimentalism over intellectuality, the shibboleths of "egalitarianism" and "democracy", and the emergence of a rampant psychologism which usurps functions which properly belong to religion. In recent times we have seen many attempts to assimilate spirituality into the domain of psychology, a move which fails to distinguish between the contingent plane of the psyche and the inviolate Self, or Spirit — this failure generating confusions of all kinds, on full display in "occultist", "New Age" and purportedly "Eastern" movements which lay claim to some kind of spirituality but which scorn traditional religious forms and practices. The same confusion can easily be discerned in the works of many modernistic writers on religious subjects, even when their general disposition towards religion is sympathetic.[3] It might also be observed in passing that it is also quite possible to be "religious" in some externalist sense — punctilious in the observation of ritual obligations and so on — yet remain quite "unspiritual"; this is the phenomenon of an empty religiosity wherein the true goals of the path have been forgotten, and all that remains is an empty husk. Such folk might usefully remember Martin Buber's remark that "it is far more comfortable to have to do with religion than to have to do with God".[4] However, even such an attenuated form of religious practice is preferable to a so-called "spirituality" which has been stripped of all sense of the Transcendent. There remains some chance that the practices which are performed only to the letter might yet re-ignite embers which seem to have died.

Traditional peoples everywhere, whatever their religious commitments, start from very different premises. To state them succinctly, and without privileging any particular theology: man is an "amphibious" or "axial" creature who lives, so to speak, between two worlds — on the one hand, the ever-changing tissue of relativities which comprise the time-space world of multiplicity and contingency ("maya" or "samsara" in the Indian lexicon), and on the other, the boundless realm of the Divine, the Absolute, God, from whence come various Revelations which provide us, in our terrestrial condition, with all things needful for our spiritual welfare and pertinent to our ultimate destiny. Such peoples could hardly conceive the idea that 'spirituality" might be an *ad hoc*, improvisatory and subjective affair; on the contrary, the God-given forms and practices of tradition (Scriptures, myths, doctrines, rituals, sacred art, moral codes and so on), the example of the saints and sages, and the guidance of those qualified to provide it (masters, lamas, directors, gurus, shamans, priests, shaykhs), provide the adherent with a detailed map of the spiritual path. It is not a matter of dreaming up a new map (which may bear little relation to the terrain to be traversed!) but of following the map which tradition invariably provides to those who seek.

In 1984 representatives of all the major religions gathered at St Benedict's Monastery in Snowmass, Colorado, to "meditate together in silence and share their personal spiritual journeys" and to deliberate on those elements of belief and practice which their traditions shared. Out of this gathering and subsequent meetings emerged a list of points of agreement. It is worth considering this list as an example of the kinds of convergences which can be discerned by adherents of different traditions working together in a spirit of cooperative fellowship and dialogue. It also throws some light on our present considerations. The Snowmass meeting proved less vaporous than many attempts at dialogue and produced the following list of elements common to all the major religions:

- The world religions bear witness to the experience of Ultimate Reality to which they give various names.
- Ultimate Reality cannot be limited by any name or concept.

- Ultimate Reality is the ground of infinite potentiality and actuality.
- Faith is opening, accepting and responding to Ultimate Reality.
- The potential for human wholeness — or in other frames of reference, enlightenment, salvation, transformation, blessedness, nirvana — is present in every human person.
- Ultimate Reality may be experienced not only through religious practices but through nature, art, human relationships and service to others.
- As long as the human condition is experienced as separate from Ultimate Reality, it is subject to ignorance and illusion, weakness and suffering.
- Disciplined practice is essential to the spiritual life. Humility, gratitude and a sense of humour are indispensable in the spiritual life.[5]

It might be observed that this register, whilst it encompasses a good deal, rather underplays the significance of tradition as the fountainhead of spiritual practice. It also somewhat marginalizes several aspects of spirituality which are fore-grounded in primordial cultures — namely, the paradigmatic function of religious mythology, the sacramental conception of the natural order, and the centrality of ritual life. Nonetheless, in the context of the Snowmass statement one may speak of "spirituality" as a disciplined practice, within the framework of an integral doctrine (derived from a Revelation), whereby we seek to realize the "infinite potentiality and actuality" of Ultimate Reality within ourselves, thus becoming conduits, so to speak, through which Divine Grace may be radiated into the world around us. Needless to say, this kind of formulation will command no assent from materialists, humanists, existentialists, and the like, not to mention those for whom the human being is nothing more than a highly evolved animal, a biological organism whose secrets will be unlocked by a materialistic science and who believe, with Francis Crick, that the soul is a fiction.[6] All that need presently be said on this front is that the whole notion of "spirituality" can have no real meaning for such people. It might be objected that there have been individuals who have experienced the deepest insights into Reality outside the cadre of any integral tradition and without any disciplined religious practice: the experience of Ramana Maharshi as a seventeen-year old — without doubt a mystical illumination of the most profound kind — might be cited as an instance. As Schuon observes, such experiences are certainly possible as a kind of "isolated miracle",[7] exceptions which prove the rule but certainly could not constitute it. In the vast majority of cases, the deepest spiritual experiences take place within the embrace of a formal religion, the soil having been prepared, so to speak, by some sort of practice as prescribed by the tradition in question. In those cases where a more or less spontaneous and quite unexpected illumination occurs, if it is to become intelligible to others and to have any efficacy in guiding them along the spiritual path, it must be assimilated into the forms (both doctrinal and practical) of the tradition in question. This, of course, is precisely what happened in the case of the Sage of Arunachala.[8] It might also be suggested that all spiritual experience is in some sense an adumbration, no matter how faint, of the mystical experience proper. One mode of spirituality is the awareness of the metaphysical transparency of every cosmic situation, awakened by what are variously called epiphanies, theophanies, hierophanies and mystical illuminations. In the theistic traditions this mode of experience is sometimes called the gift of "seeing God everywhere" — but it is a universal phenomena and one dramatically exemplified by those many saints and sages who perceive the transcendent dimension which is "hidden" in all natural phenomena. One may cite as representative examples such figures as Rumi, St Francis of Assisi, St Seraphim of Sarov, Ramakrishna and Black Elk.

To conclude: "spirituality" *in vacuo* is indeed a vacuous notion! If the term is to have any meaning and vitality it must be understood within the framework of a religious tradition. In its most simple formulation, spirituality is to do with shattering the fetters of the ego (in Sufi terms, the taming of the *nafs*), the submission of the human will to the Will of Heaven, the "alchemical" transformation of the soul and, in the language of the Vedanta, the re-discovery of that Self (Atman) which Alone is Real. All of this lies infinitely beyond the scope of any profane science; nor can it be accommodated in those pseudo-spiritual and humanistic counterfeits which claim to dispense with the dictates of tradition.

NOTES ON COSMIC CYCLES
AND THE KALI YUGA

...our age...marks the end of a great cyclic period of terrestrial humanity...and so must recapitulate or manifest again in one way or another everything that is included in the cycle, in conformity with the adage 'extremes meet'.

– Frithjof Schuon[1]

...the doctrine of the Kali-Yuga and the Kalki-Avatāra — the 'dark age' and the 'universal Messiah' — [is] a doctrine whose importance is such that no Revelation can ignore it, whatever its symbolism, which is to say that it constitutes a criterion of orthodoxy and thereby of spiritual purity and wholeness. Since this truth, which is Christian as well as Hindu, being indeed found everywhere, excludes evolutionism, it is a bulwark of tradition against the most pernicious errors...

– Frithjof Schuon[2]

H ERE IS the opening passage of René Guénon's *Crisis of the Modern World* (1927):

> The Hindu doctrine teaches that a human cycle, to which it gives the name *Manvantara*, is divided into four periods marking so many stages during which the primordial spirituality gradually becomes more and more obscured; these periods correspond with the Golden, Silver, Bronze and iron Ages of the ancient Western traditions. We are now in the fourth age, the *Kali-Yuga* or 'dark age', and have been so already, it is said, for more than six thousand years...Since that time, the truths which formerly lay within reach of all mankind have now become more and more hidden and difficult of approach...it is also stated that what is thus hidden will become visible again at the end of our cycle, which, by reason of the continuity linking all things together, will coincide with the beginning of a new cycle.[3]

Some of the principal themes of Guénon's later writings unfold in the light of the doctrine of cycles, one which is most clearly expounded within the Indian tradition but is to be found in one form or another virtually everywhere in traditional worlds. The doctrine provides the context for Guénon's exposure of the 'solidification' and 'materialization' whereby humankind becomes increasingly impervious to beneficent spiritual influences from above and, by the same token, increasingly vulnerable to infernal influences from below (psychism being a case in point). Guénon is also at pains to point out that because man and the cosmos itself are reciprocally influenced then the same process of degeneration so clearly evident in man himself is also taking place, simultaneously, in the terrestrial environment. This is all of a piece with Guénon's anatomization of the "signs of the times" and his ruthless critique of modernity in all its bizarre guises. In contrast, one does not find in Frithjof Schuon's writings any sustained exposition of this doctrine, nor many references to the Kali Yuga, the Iron Age in which mankind has long since been living. Nonetheless, it is clear that Schuon is familiar with the Hindu sources; furthermore, he is familiar with a range of Indian sources concerning cycles, including the *Manava-Dharma-Shastra* and several Puranas of which the Frenchman was apparently unaware.[4] No doubt there are good reasons for Schuon's comparative reticence on this subject — amongst them his eschewal of historicism of all kinds. As he remarks in one of his essays, "it is not normally our practice to enter into the details of historical or personal phenomena".[5] Nonetheless, it is clear that this doctrine informs Schuon's understanding of time, his sense of terrestrial and human history as a whole and his understanding of the "end times" in which we find ourselves. It is also perfectly clear from his writings that Schuon, like Guénon, is keenly aware of the imminent end of the current cycle. In *The Feathered Sun* (1990) we find this: "The writer of these lines knows that the present world will come to an end, in a future which is not far off."[6] It is not our purpose here to explicate this doctrine nor to consider its manifold applications and ramifications.[7] Rather we shall touch on a few aspects of the doctrine especially pertinent to Schuon's work. However, before that, a few general remarks.

Firstly, it is perhaps useful to point out that the doctrine is both metaphysical and cosmological, which is to say that it is concerned both with those ultimate realities which lie "outside" time and space (metaphysics), and, in the light of that Science of the Real, with the various time-space relativities which comprise the universe in both its subtle and gross aspects (cosmology). It might also be said, recalling our discussion of the Five Divine Presences, that the doctrine also pertains to that which lies "between" the divine Principle and the manifested world. All of this is nicely, and precisely, summed up in this passage from Schuon:

> Basically, metaphysical doctrine is nothing other than the science of reality and illusion, and it presents itself, from the starting-point of the terrestrial state — and thus with its cosmological extension — as the science of the existential or principial degrees, as the case may be: on the one hand, it distinguishes within the principle itself between Being and non-Being, or in other words between the personal God and the impersonal Divinity; on the other hand, within manifestation, metaphysics — now become cosmology — distinguishes between the formless and the formal, the latter being in turn divided into two states, the one subtle or animic and the other gross or corporeal.[8]

The doctrine of cycles, in no matter which religious context we find it, is antithetical to the views of time and history which have so tyrannized the modern mentality, mesmerized as it is by ideas of "evolution" and "progress". It concerns the unfolding of various terrestrial and cosmic cycles without an understanding of which we are quite unable to discern the larger, transhistorical forces at work throughout human history — for the moment leaving aside the awesome mysteries of time and space as they are writ on the universe at large. One Indian scholar has summarized the Hindu understanding of the cosmological process this way: "manifestation from the unmanifest, gradual unfoldment, involution in the reverse sequence, and final dissolution in the original source".[9] In brief, everything "comes from" Brahman and everything "returns" thither.

In *The Reign of Quantity* Guénon alludes frequently to the Hindu expression of the doctrine; the whole work is pervaded by a sense of the inevitable cataclysms which close the present terrestrial cycle and bring this world to an end. Other perennialists, particularly Martin Lings, have also written about the "eleventh hour" and the "latter days" to which so many traditions allude. However, this is a domain into which one should venture with great caution; it is all too easy to get lost in endless speculations about the precise duration of the ages and in fruitless attempts to determine exactly where we might stand with regard to the Last Days. All too often we end up with a jumble of traditional images and symbols, wrenched out of context and forcibly married to a historicist understanding of time and history, one quite impervious to various considerations which would make the traditional doctrines more intelligible — the extravagant and characteristically Indian penchant for the hyperbolic use of number, for instance, or the privileging of myth over history, or, indeed, the recondite symbolism of numbers themselves. More often than not the method of analysis and interpretation is altogether inadequate to the material at hand. This is but one of many fields where "the reign of quantity" has obscured any real understanding. (An analogous case might be the confusion evident in the belief that one can "explain" meditative states by clamping to the meditator's head a jungle of wires connected to a computer!) It hardly need be added that when the spiritually immature are exposed to doctrines concerning the end of the world, then all manner of incongruous results may well be expected. With all this in mind we will not be surprised by

Seyyed Hossein Nasr's somewhat terse remark, at a conference on tradition and modernity in 2006, that among perennialists themselves "there are far too many 'experts' on the Kali Yuga!"

One of the sayings of the Prophet Mohammad: "No time cometh upon you but is followed by a worse".[10] As we have seen when considering the relationship of a religious tradition to its origin in a divine Revelation, the traditional outlook generally supposes that the best of worlds was "in the beginning", at the moment of creation, and that thereafter follows a long process of decline and degeneration. In the frame of human history this process can be most clearly seen in the spiritual radiance which shines forth from the moment of a particular Revelation, inevitably followed, over time, by humankind's increasing indifference to the messages vouchsafed by the tradition which has issued from that Revelation, their neglect of those teachings and values which their ancestors held dear, their increasing ensnarement in ephemeralities and superficialities, their forgetfulness, and their "descent" into matter. In previous ages, a different spiritual and material order obtained, one quite unintelligible — indeed, impenetrable — to a scientistic mentality which, on the one hand, is more or less completely ignorant of the supra-corporeal dimensions of reality and the "multiple states of being" which those dimensions encompass, and, on the other, is locked into a horizontal and quantitative understanding of time and an evolutionistic view of history. To adduce one instance of a feature of earlier ages which is now beyond the grasp of both "science" and "history" — simple enough but with far-reaching implications — one need only refer to the fact that previously, in Schuon's words, "The partition between the material and animic states was not yet 'hardened' or 'congealed' as is above all the case in our own epoch".[11] And to go one step further, to demonstrate how an ignorance of metaphysical and cosmological principles plays itself out even in the reading of the "material evidence", consider the implications of the whole process of "materialization" (as mapped by Guénon) in the context of evolutionary theory. In his magisterial essay on traditional cosmology and modern science Titus Burckhardt does just this. After surveying and juxtaposing traditional cosmogonies and Darwinian evolution, he observes that:

> It is certain that the process of materialization, going from supersensory to sensory, had to be reflected within the material or corporeal state itself, so that one is on safe ground in saying that the first generations of a new species did not leave their mark in the great book of earthly layering; it is therefore useless to want to seek in sensible matter the ancestors of a species and especially those of man.[12]

Whilst on the subject of evolutionism, it is worth remarking that Schuon has affirmed that while the doctrine of the Kali Yuga and the *Kalki-Avatāra* is one most readily found in the Hindu and Christian traditions (the latter clothing the doctrine in a different symbolic vocabulary), its "importance is such that no Revelation can ignore it, whatever its symbolism". The doctrine manifestly excludes evolutionism as a universal principle or as an over-arching explanatory theory:

> We do not deny that evolution exists within certain limits, as is indeed evident enough, but we do deny that it is a universal principle, hence a law that affects and determines all things, including the immutable; evolution and degeneration can moreover go hand in hand, each then occurring on a different

plane. Be that as it may, what has to be categorically rejected is the idea that truth evolves or that revealed doctrines are the product of an evolution.[13]

It is no accident that the world's religious mythologies are replete with stories of a Fall of some kind; the dramatic allegorical narratives — myths — of peoples from around the globe testify to a more or less universal intuition of the principle that "things go downhill". The principle might most succinctly be summed up this way: creation-deterioration-dissolution. As Guénon observes, "the development of anything that is manifested will necessarily imply a gradual accelerating movement away from the principle whence it originates".[14] This motif is clearly evident, for example, in the Old Testament accounts of the Creation, the Fall, the Flood and the Tower of Babel. The principle is given rich symbolic expression in various myths about the different ages, usually four in number and most commonly associated with the metals gold, silver, bronze and iron. Both the mythological and metaphysical expressions of the principle find their richest expressions in the Hindu tradition, though analogous narratives and doctrines are to be found everywhere (although sometimes heavily veiled, for reasons to which some allusion has already been made). In the case of Schuon's *oeuvre*, the doctrine perhaps comes closest to the surface in his writings about the American Indians; for instance, in "His Holiness and the Medicine Man" in *The Feathered Sun*, Schuon draws attention to the parallelism of the buffalo and the bull in the respective symbolic vocabularies of the Plains Indians and the Hindus:

A most striking feature of the North American branch of the Primordial Sanatana Dharma is the doctrine of the four yugas: the sacred animal of the Plains Indians, the buffalo, symbolizes the *mahāyuga* [the great age or cycle], each of its legs representing a yuga [an age within the cycle]. At the beginning of this *mahāyuga* a buffalo was placed by the Great spirit at the West in order to hold back the waters which menace the earth; every year this bison loses a hair, and in every yuga it loses a foot. When it will have lost all its hair and its feet, the waters will overwhelm the earth and the *mahāyuga* will be finished. The analogy with the bull of Dharma in Hinduism is very remarkable; at every yuga, this bull withdraws a foot, and spirituality loses its strength; and now we are near the end of the *kali-yuga*.

And lest we be in any doubt as to the authenticity of the doctrines embedded in this mythic imagery, Schuon goes on to add this:

> Like the orthodox Hindus, the traditional Red Indians have this conviction [of our proximity to the end of the Kali-Yuga] which is obviously true in spite of all the mundane optimism of the modern world; but let us add that the compensation of our very dark age is the Mercy of the Holy Name, as it is emphasized in the *Manava-Dharma Shastra* and the *Shrimad Bhagavata* and other holy scriptures.[15]

Here is how the Vishnu Purana, a Hindu text dating back nearly two millennia, envisages the degenerations which can be expected in the latter days of the Kali Yuga:

> Riches and piety will diminish daily, until the world will be completely corrupted. In those days it will be wealth that confers distinction, passion will be the sole reason for union

between the sexes, lies will be the only method of success in business, and women will be the objects merely of sensual gratification. The earth will be valued only for its mineral treasures, dishonesty will be the universal means of subsistence, a simple ablution will be regarded as sufficient purification... The observances of castes, laws, and institutions will no longer be in force in the Dark Age, and the ceremonies prescribed by the Vedas will be neglected. Women will obey only their whims and will be infatuated with pleasure...men of all kinds will presumptuously regard themselves as equals of Brahmins [priests, scholars]...The Vaishyas [merchants and farmers] will abandon agriculture and commerce and will earn their living by servitude or by the exercise of mechanical professions...The dominant caste will be that of the Shudras [workers]...[16]

No one of any spiritual discernment can fail to be struck by the chilling accuracy of this passage as a description of our present circumstances. As Guénon remarked

By all traditional data we know that we have been in the Kali Yuga for a long time already; and we can say without fear of error that we are in an advanced phase, a phase whose description in the Puranas corresponds in the most striking fashion to the characteristics of our present epoch.[17]

As William Stoddart has noted, this Puranic has a close parallel in the writings of the Apostle:

In the last days, perilous times shall come: men will love nothing but money and self; they will be arrogant, boastful and abusive, with no respect for parents, no gratitude, no piety, no natural affection...They will be men who put pleasure in the place of God, who preserve the outward form of religion, but are a standing denial of its reality...Ever learning, but never able to come to a knowledge of the truth.[18]

No civilization is immune to the ravages of the Kali Yuga but Schuon reminds us that there is a significant difference between a falling away from traditional wisdom, such as can today be observed almost anywhere in the East, and its complete repudiation — either by explicit denial or, perhaps more commonly, by neglect — which, amongst the so-called intelligentsia at least, has been the hallmark of the modern West:

> The Oriental civilizations, in their cyclical decadence, have more or less disfigured or corrupted the principles; modern Western civilization denies them, which amounts to killing the patient in order to cure the disease; the *kali-yuga* is everywhere.[19]

Our understanding of the doctrine of cycles will be precarious if it is not also realized that there are cycles within cycles: each civilization, each tradition, will itself go through cycles which echo the greater cosmic rhythms on a smaller temporal scale. Furthermore, the appearance of an avatar, or even a great saint or sage, or some other divinely-initiated event, may well inaugurate a "golden age" within the tradition which yet remains subject to those greater degenerations whose patterns can only be seen from a distant vantage-point. It is in the nature of things that any particular period in human history will necessarily exhibit both "ascents" (returning to the principle) and "descents" (falling away from the principle), both centripetal and centrifugal tendencies. In other words, there are oscillations, alternations and modulations in Time itself, an understanding of which precludes those over-simplifications which often characterize both linear and cyclic "philosophies" of history. One sympathizes with the Rumanian philosopher E. M. Cioran when he writes, "Out in the street, suddenly overcome by the 'mystery' of Time, I told myself that Saint Augustine was quite right to deal with such a theme by addressing himself directly to God: with whom else to discuss it?"[20]

It might also be useful to remark in passing that if the doctrine of cycles is to be protected from the corrosive effects of a reductionist historicism we cannot too often repeat that it is only the relative dimensions of Reality which are in any way subject to the vicissitudes of time. One of the abiding principles of the *sophia perennis* is that of aeviternity, in Eliade's words "the eternal intemporal present".[21] A succinct statement of the principle comes from Aquinas: "there is no before or after to be reckoned with in constant changeless Reality...the now of time is not time: the now of eternity is really the same as eternity."[22] But all this is beyond the ken of an outlook in which Time has been flattened out into nothing more than a horizontal duration. Accompanying this "flattening" has been the rise of historicism and the more or less obsessive recording of the minutiae of our temporal existence, paralleling the relentless drive of science to accumulate ever more empirical data — as if understanding could ever be based on mere aggregation! Nor is the rise of historicism without its ironies. Mircea Eliade has suggested that modern man's almost phobic fixation on history — which from a metaphysical viewpoint is an "aspect", so to speak, of *maya*, and thus possessing no more than a contingent reality — might parallel the dying man's re-living of his life in all its particularities, and thus be a sign (seen only by the few) that we are indeed rapidly approaching the end times.[23] "History", after all, is but "the rhythm of universal decadence".[24]

✳

We live in anomalous times. Nowhere is this more graphically demonstrated than in the fact that in the most irreligious and impious period in human history the esoteric wisdoms preserved by the religious traditions are more widely and easily accessible than ever before. Sapiential truths which previously had remained extrinsically inexpressible and which had been protected by those few capable of understanding them are now on public display, as it were. The perennialists themselves have played a significant role in bringing esoteric wisdoms within the purview of a greater number of people. This calls for some explanation.

The erosion of the protective barriers which previously enclosed traditions has, in part, been caused by historical factors which, in a sense, are "accidental". One might cite the exposure of the Upanisadic Scriptures as a case in point; here certain historical factors, such as the introduction into India of cheap printing presses, combined with a degree of imprudence on the part of some of the "reformers" of Hinduism to subvert the esoteric status of these Scriptures which were made available to anyone and everyone. There are also innumerable cases where a garbled version of half-understood secret doctrines has been thoughtlessly and carelessly put into public circulation. The Biblical verse "For there is nothing covered, that shall not be revealed..." (Luke 12:2) has sometimes been taken as a license for all manner of excesses in the popularizing of esoteric doctrines. The warnings about false prophets might often be more to the point.

In the case of the traditionalists the unveiling of some esoteric teachings has been considered and prudent. What sorts of factors have allowed this development? Firstly, there are certain cosmic and cyclic conditions now obtaining which make for an unprecedented situation. In discussing the fact that what was once hid in the darkness is now being brought into the light, Schuon writes:

> there is indeed something abnormal in this, but it lies, not in the fact of the exposition of these truths, but in the general conditions of our age, which marks the end of a great cyclic period of terrestrial humanity — the end of a *mahāyuga* according to Hindu cosmology — and so must recapitulate or manifest again in one way or another everything that is included in the cycle, in conformity with the adage "extremes meet"; thus things that are in themselves abnormal may become necessary by reason of the conditions just referred to.[25]

Secondly, from a more expedient point of view,

> ...it must be admitted that the spiritual confusion of our times has reached such a pitch that the harm that might in principle befall certain people from contact with the truths in question is compensated by the advantages that others will derive from the self-same truths.[26]

Schuon reminds us of the Kabbalistic adage that "it is better to divulge Wisdom than to forget it."[27] And thirdly there is the fact already mentioned: esoteric doctrines have, in recent times, been so frequently "plagiarized and deformed" that those who are in a position to speak with authority on these matters are obliged to give some account of what "true esoterism is and what it is not".[28]

From another perspective it can be said that the preservation, indeed the very survival, of the formal exoterisms may depend on the revivifying effects of an esoterism more widely understood:

> exoterism is a precarious thing by reason of its limits or its exclusions: there arrives a moment in history when all kinds of experiences oblige it to modify its claims to exclusiveness, and it is then driven to a choice: escape from these limitations by the upward path, in esoterism, or by the downward path, in a worldly and suicidal liberalism.[29]

At a time when "the outward and readily exaggerated incompatibility of the different religions greatly discredits, in the minds of most of our contemporaries, all religion",[30] the exposure of the underlying unity of the religions takes on a deep urgency. This task can only be achieved through esoterism. The open confrontation of different exoterisms, the extirpation of traditional civilizations, and the tyranny of secular and profane ideologies are symptomatic of the cyclical conditions; all play a part in determining the peculiar circumstances in which the most imperious needs of the age can only be answered by a recourse to traditional esoterisms. There is perhaps some small hope that in this climate and given a properly constituted metaphysical framework in which to affirm the "profound and eternal solidarity of all spiritual forms",[31] the different religions might yet "present a singular front against the floodtide of materialism and pseudo-spiritualism".[32]

The hazards and ambiguities attending the exposure of esoteric doctrines to an audience in many respects ill-equipped to understand them have posed the same problems for representatives of traditional esoterisms the world over. Joseph Epes Brown writes of the disclosure of traditional Lakota wisdom, to choose one example, in terms very similar to those used by Schuon:

> ...in these days those few old wise men still living among them say that at the approach of the end of a cycle, when men everywhere have become unfit to understand and still more to realize the truths revealed to them at the origin...it is then permissible and even desirable to bring this knowledge out into the light of day, for by its own nature truth protects itself against being profaned and in this way it is possible it may reach those qualified to penetrate it deeply.[33]

It is no accident that the few remaining holy men amongst the American Indians and traditionalists like Schuon should see this matter in the same terms.

✳

At a time when the forces of anti-Tradition sometimes seem overwhelming and when we feel unable to keep our hands to the plough, let us recall Frithjof Schuon's reminder that no effort on behalf of the Truth is ever in vain.[34] We must dispel the false charges sometimes leveled at traditionalists that they are dusty obscurantists "out of touch" with the contemporary world, that they want to "wind back the clock", that they are romantic reactionaries escaping into an idealized past. Let us never forget that the essential message of Tradition is timeless and thus ever new, ever fresh, and always germane to both our immediate condition and to our ultimate destiny. As Schuon remarks, a "nostalgia for the past" is, in itself, nothing; all that is meaningful is "a nostalgia for the sacred" which "cannot be situated elsewhere than in the liberating 'now' of God".[35] No doubt our crepuscular era is riddled with all manner of confusion but there are always saints and sages in our midst to whom we can turn for guidance. In recent times one might mention such figures as the Algerian Sufi master, Shaykh Ahmed Al Alawi, or Hindu sages such as Paramahamsa Ramakrishna, Ramana Maharshi and Anandamayi, or Native American visionaries such as Black Elk and Yellowtail, or the Christian monk, Henri Le Saux who became Swami Abhishiktananda, not to mention the many wise lamas and masters of the Far Eastern world, including such persons as His Holiness the Dalai Lama and Thich Nhat Hanh. Then, too, there is the abiding work and example of the great perennialists. By way of a final observation on the cyclic conditions now obtaining we can take note of a recurrent theme in Schuon's writings on spirituality: the peculiar efficacy, in the latter days, of the Invocation of the Holy Name. This is a "saving barque" to which we can cling when nearly everything else of the spiritual order has been lost to sight. "Whoever shall call upon the Name of the Lord shall be saved."[36] These words of St Paul take on new weight and urgency at this juncture in history.

TO A BUDDHIST BEAT

ALLEN GINSBERG ON POLITICS, POETICS AND SPIRITUALITY

What we [the Beats] were proposing was some new sense of spiritual consciousness. We were interested in non-violence, sexual freedom, the exploration of psychedelic drugs and sensitivity. We were aware that the entire government...was corrupt. We were interested in Eastern thought and meditation. We had quite an open heart and open mind...

– Allen Ginsberg[1]

Every era has to reinvent the project of "spirituality" for itself...In the modern era one of the most active metaphors for the spiritual project is "art"...a particularly adaptable site on which to stage the formal dramas besetting consciousness, each individual work of art being a more or less astute paradigm for regulating or reconciling these contradictions...

– Susan Sontag[2]

INTRODUCTION

O N M AY 6, 1972, Allen Ginsberg took the Three Refuges
of Buddhism. At a ceremony in the Dharmadhatu
Meditation Center in Boulder, Colorado, Ginsberg — disaffected
Jew, Beat poet, counter culture eminence, gay spokesman,
teacher, itinerant bard, political dissident, prankster — pledged
to take refuge in the Buddha, the dharma (Buddhist teachings)
and the sangha (the Buddhist community). In addition he took
the Bodhisattva vows which committed him, in the face of
inexhaustible obstacles, to work ceaselessly for the liberation of
all sentient beings. As part of the ceremony Ginsberg accepted his
refuge name of "Dharma Lion", bestowed by his Tibetan guru,
Chögyam Trungpa Rinpoche.[3] This consummated an interest in
Buddhism going back to the early 50s. Until his death in April
1997 Ginsberg remained committed to the Buddhist path, and
devoted a good deal of his exuberant energies to dharma work.
For most of the rest of his life he sat in meditation for at least an
hour a day and did many extended retreats in which he underwent
advanced training in various Buddhist disciplines. He worked
enthusiastically on behalf of several Buddhist organizations,
particularly the Naropa Institute in Boulder and, in his later
years, the Jewel Heart Center in Ann Arbor, Michigan.

Ginsberg's death occasioned much comment on his role in
American letters and in the cultural disturbances of the last
four decades but, outside the organs of the American Buddhist
community, surprisingly little notice was directed to Ginsberg's
engagement with Eastern forms of spirituality. Ginsberg's public
career and private life (a somewhat slippery distinction in his
case!) have been documented in prodigious detail by two recent
biographers.[4] There is no point in rehearsing that story here;

rather, I want to reflect on his encounter with Asian religious forms. Ginsberg's life and work might be seen as an exemplary site on which various convergences and syntheses take place. Most notably perhaps, we can discern a creative fusion of various polarities and categorizations — East and West, the sacred and profane, the religious and the political, the intellectual and the sensual, the spiritual and the aesthetic.

GINSBERG'S SPIRITUAL TRAJECTORY

In retracing his own spiritual growth Ginsberg invariably referred to a pivotal experience in the summer of 1948. At the time he was an undergraduate at Columbia, studying under Lionel Trilling and Mark van Doren, and living in East Harlem. He had already met both William Burroughs and Jack Kerouac with whom he spent a good deal of time discussing "new consciousness", smoking dope, and experimenting with literary forms which might best capture "the texture of consciousness" (one of Ginsberg's favourite phrases). He had also embarked on a wide-ranging exploration of the mystical literature of the West, particularly Plotinus, St John of the Cross, St Teresa of Avila, Marvell and Blake. Here is one of Ginsberg's many accounts of the experience:

> ...on the sixth floor of a Harlem tenement on 121st Street looking out at the roofs while reading Blake, back and forth, [I] suddenly had an auditory hallucination, hearing Blake — what I thought was his voice, very deep, earthen tone, not very far from my own mature tone of voice...reciting a poem called "The Sunflower," which I thought expressed some kind of universal longing for union with some infinite nature...I

looked out the window and began to notice the extraordinary detail of the intelligent labor that had gone into the making of the rooftop cornices...And I suddenly realized that the world was, in a sense, not dead matter, but an increment or deposit of living intelligence and action and activity that finally took form...And as I looked at the sky I wondered what kind of intelligence had made that vastness, or what was the nature of the intelligence that I was glimpsing, and felt a sense of vastness and of coming home to a space I hadn't realized was there before but which seemed old and infinite, like the ancient of Days, so to speak.[5]

In a much earlier account Ginsberg described the voice in these terms: "The peculiar quality of the voice was something unforgettable because it was like God had a human voice, with all the infinite tenderness and mortal gravity of a living Creator speaking to his son".[6] Elsewhere he called the experience a "beatific illumination" in which he "saw the universe unfold in my brain".[7]

Several other intense experiences, each linked to one of Blake's poems, ensued in the following weeks. All the while Ginsberg was experimenting with drugs — marijuana, peyote, mescalin, later LSD — though no drug-induced experience left as deep an imprint as "The Sunflower" episode. In his researches into Zen Buddhism in the early 50s Ginsberg was struck by the apparent affinities between his own experience and *satori* as described by D.T. Suzuki and others. In fact, Ginsberg remained preoccupied with recreating this experience for the next fifteen years, only snapping out of what he described as a kind of stupefaction during a meeting in India with Dudjom Rinpoche, head of the Nyingma branch of Tibetan Buddhism. The Rinpoche's adjuration to forego clinging to experiences, whether pleasant or unpleasant, struck home.[8]

In the early 50s Kerouac introduced Ginsberg to several Buddhist texts, singing passages from Sanskrit sutras *à la* Frank Sinatra *circa* 1952.[9] Ginsberg's initial reactions to the rudimentary teachings of the Buddha are interesting:

> as an ex-Communist Jewish intellectual, I thought his pronouncement of the First Noble Truth, that existence was suffering, was some sort of insult to my left-wing background, since I was a progressive looking forward to the universal improvement of matters...[10]

Ginsberg tells us that it took him two years to accept Kerouac's insistence that the First Noble Truth was "a very simple fact". Also crucial to Ginsberg's initiation into the world of Eastern spirituality was his discovery of Chinese painting in the Fine Arts Room of the New York Public Library, an interest in Tibetan iconography (particularly the "horrific deities") and the *Book of the Dead*. This triggered a lot of "new mind and eyeball kicks" and inaugurated a massive reading program which included D.T. Suzuki's seminal *Introduction to Zen Buddhism* (1934).[11]

By 1962 Ginsberg, now probably the best-known and certainly the most controversial poet in America, felt the need for a spiritual teacher sufficiently acutely to go on an extended visit to India with his friend and fellow poet Gary Snyder. Although he visited many holy sites and met a range of distinguished spiritual leaders and teachers (including Swami Shivananda, Dudjom Rinpoche, Gyalwa Karmapa, and the Dalai Lama) Ginsberg did not attach himself to any particular guru nor commit himself to any specific spiritual method.[12] An eclectic mixture of the

Hindu and the Buddhist, haphazard meditation of one kind and another, mantra chanting and more drugs remained the order of the day. It was not until 1970 that Swami Muktananda introduced Ginsberg to a systematic meditation practice. However, it was to be Chögyam Trungpa, met briefly in India in 1962, who was to become Ginsberg's guru.

Trungpa was a highly charismatic and controversial figure in American Buddhism. Born in Tibet in 1939, he was identified as a tulku (reincarnation of an enlightened teacher) at thirteen months and underwent the intensive Tibetan training culminating in full ordination in the Kagyu sect at the age of eighteen. After a highly dramatic escape from Tibet following the Chinese invasion, and a period in India, Trungpa had gone to Oxford to study philosophy, comparative religion and fine art before setting up the Samye-Ling Meditation Center in Scotland. Some years later he moved to America and was the prime mover in establishing the Naropa Institute in Boulder, Colorado.[13] He was to have a profound impact on Ginsberg — so much so that Ginsberg was later to say that, "he left such an imprint on my consciousness that I in a sense see through his eyes or see through the same eyes of those occasions where he pointed direction to me."[14]

After an apparently chance encounter in a New York street in 1970, Trungpa and Ginsberg developed a close and complex relationship: guru and *chela*, philosophical sparring partners, drinking buddies, fellow poets, tricksters, kindred spirits. Under the Tibetan's invitation Ginsberg, with Anne Waldman, set up the Jack Kerouac School of Disembodied Poetics within the Naropa Institute. For many years Ginsberg taught a summer school there which explored the connections between meditation and poetry: "the life of meditation and the life of art," he claimed, "are both based on a similar conception of spontaneous mind. They both share renunciation as a way of avoiding a conditioned art work, or trite art, or repetition of other people's ideas."[15] Under Trungpa's guidance, he also developed his own meditational practice and deepened his understanding of the *Vajrayāna* tradition in particular (though he retained an interest in Zen Buddhism and Hinduism, as well as later turning back to the Judaism which was his patrimony). It was Trungpa who persuaded Ginsberg to perform improvisational poetry.

From the early 70s onwards Ginsberg could properly be described as a serious Buddhist practitioner: as one observer noted in 1976, "classical Buddhist practice has become the core of Ginsberg's life".[16] Three years after Trungpa's death in 1986 Philip Glass introduced Ginsberg to another Tibetan master with whom he also developed a close relationship — Kyabje Gelek Rinpoche of the Gelugpa sect, based at the Jewel Heart Center in Ann Arbor, Michigan. Ginsberg himself has noted how the intense devotion and desire which he had previously directed to his literary heroes, friends and multifarious lovers — often to no very good effect — was now largely transferred to the dharma and the guru.[17]

Some of the attractions of Buddhism for one of Ginsberg's temperament and experience are plain enough. Buddhism offered a spiritual therapy which could address his deep psychic wounds. Buddhist teachings and meditational practice certainly helped Ginsberg to at least partially heal some of the deep-seated confusions and anxieties, "elements of resentment, aggression and dead-end anger" which were the legacy of a painful and traumatic childhood. He never lost his sharp sense of life's absurdities but increasingly understood the pain and pathos of the condition to which the Buddha's First Noble Truth alerts us. The form of Buddhism espoused by Trungpa was pragmatic and experiential in method, doctrinally "open", and free of any disabling associations with either conservative politics or puritanical moralism. Buddhism's non-theistic metaphysic appealed to Ginsberg's anti-authoritarian personality ("there is no Central Intelligence Agency in the universe") and provided a vocabulary in which he could better understand the epiphanies of his student days.[18]

By way of an aside we might note that Ginsberg's various involvements with Tibetan Buddhist organizations in the 70s and 80s, and the controversies and tensions in which he often found himself involved — most notably the "Naropa Poetry Wars"[19] — illuminate several aspects of the "Americanizing" of the *Vajrayāna*. Jack Kornfield has identified democratization (the disassembling of patriarchal and authoritarian power structures, and the move from a monastic to a lay orientation), feminization (the inclusion of women at all levels of practice and leadership), and integration (the adaptation of Buddhist practice to the exigencies of everyday lay life in late 20th century America) as the three key changes in this process.[20] Another conspicuous motif in the development of American Buddhism is the rapid emergence of what has come to be called "engaged Buddhism", one dynamically and directly concerned with the most pressing socio-political issues of the day.[21]

Of the many ceremonies that marked Allen Ginsberg's death the Jewel Heart Memorial Service at Ann Arbor was especially poignant. The religious service included both Tibetan and Jewish chants and prayers, and was followed by a concert of poetry and music, read or sung by Ann Waldman, Bob Rosenthal (Ginsberg's personal secretary), Natalie Merchant and Patti Smith, and including works by Ginsberg, Kerouac and Bob Dylan. The San Francisco ceremony at the Temple Emmanuel included tributes from Snyder, Diane Di Prima, Lawrence Ferlinghetti, Robert Hass, Joanne Kryger and Andrew Schelling.[22]

POLITICS, POETICS AND THE WESTERN ENCOUNTER WITH EASTERN SPIRITUALITY

Several questions arise. As the old song has it, "What's it all about Alfie?" How did this encounter with Buddhism impact on Ginsberg's politics, his aesthetics and his worldview generally? In the context of American cultural transformations what might Ginsberg's experience exemplify? What might we learn from this engagement about the nature of the American experience of Tibetan Buddhism in the second half of the 20th century? What kind of "divides" did Ginsberg traverse and wherein lies the significance of his spiritual migrations? I do not wish to essay answers to these questions in any very systematic or exhaustive way but rather to offer a few observations which touch on them at various points.

Ginsberg's persona and his place in the collective American psyche probably has as much to do with his role as a political gadfly as poet — and indeed he would not have separated the two. From the early Columbia days right down to his death Ginsberg was a burr under the saddle of conservative America, constantly mocking bourgeois values and scandalizing the burghers, puncturing uncomfortable hypocrisies and exposing corruption in the body politic. With his own inimitable mixture of insouciance, outré charm, moral gravity and impassioned eloquence he championed causes such as the protection of free expression, gay rights, the ending of the Vietnam War, ecological awareness, the unmasking of American imperialism. All of this is quite unexceptional. What is interesting in this context is the way in which Ginsberg's career fuses spiritual and political values, and creates a style and vocabulary of political critique which owes much more to the prophets of ancient Israel, Blake, and Thoreau than to, say, Marx, Bakunin, Goldman, or indeed to Mill, the Webbs or G.B. Shaw. He had little time for the confrontationist and angry slogans of the SDS and the Weathermen and believed that the rather facile politicization of youth much in evidence in the 60s had somewhat undermined the Beat impulses towards spiritual liberation.[23]

> Interviewer: Kenneth Rexroth deemed you "a poet of revolt"... are you still?

> Ginsberg: I never have been a poet of revolt, never never never. That's saying you want to become wiser by becoming dumber, you want to become more peaceful by getting angry. ...My interest is in alteration in consciousness, in new vision... goes back to 1945 conversations with Kerouac. Revolt of consciousness, ok.[24]

> Interviewer: How have you been active in fighting for gay rights?

> Ginsberg: I don't believe in fighting.[25]

European radicalism since the 18th century has been, in the main, fiercely secular and militantly atheistic. Institutional religion has been seen, more often than not, as an oppressive and reactionary force and notions of the "spiritual" and "mystical" have been variously stigmatized as superstition, obscurantism, alienation, cowardice and neurosis. It is no surprise that Ginsberg should align himself, emotionally and intellectually, with the one significant group of political radicals who did not accept the materialistic, positivistic and progressivist assumptions of the Enlightenment, namely the Romantic poets. Nor is it an accident that Romantic values should have figured so largely, though often in caricature, in the counter culture of the 60s. What the counter culture offered was, in Theodore Roszak's word's, "a defection from the long-standing tradition of skeptical, secular intellectuality which has served as the prime vehicle for three hundred years of scientific and technical work in the West".[26] Ginsberg's principal role as counter-cultural figure was as a "vagabond proselytizer" of a this-wordly mysticism, "an ecstasy of the body and the earth that somehow embraces and transforms mortality...a joy that includes...the commonplace obscenities of our existence".[27]

Ginsberg's "beatific illuminations" and his subsequent immersion in Indian, Tibetan and Japanese spirituality gave him a perspective and a metaphysic which certainly did not blunt his political radicalism but which provided a certain distance, a sense of proportion, and a scale of values which moved him past an adolescent rage at the cultural wasteland of Ike and Dale Carnegie and Lassie, and the "Single Vision" of a materialistic gospel of progress, took him beyond the narrow, antagonistic dichotomies of Marxist rhetoric and the easy sentimentalities of Utopianism in its manifold guises. Increasingly his political stance, and indeed his poetry, seemed to derive less from the impulse to mockery, from hatred and alienation, and more from a sense of compassion, remembering that in the Buddhist context compassion (*karuna*) is inseparable from wisdom (*prajna*) of which it is actually the dynamic aspect. Ginsberg's later interviews often evince the non-combative and compassionate values which lie at the heart of the Buddhist tradition.

In a larger context we might ponder the significance of the changes whereby the iconic figures of the secular left (say Lenin, Emma Goldman, Trotsky, Joe Hill) have lost a good deal of their lustre whilst those whose radicalism is governed by a "politics of eternity" (say Gandhi, Martin Luther King, the Dalai Lama) take on a new aura. This answers to something much deeper than the whimsies of political fashion. It is tempting to believe that a new paradigm of socio-political transformation is still being fashioned, one drawing on the European post-Enlightenment, radical mainstream but discarding its one-dimensional materialism and utilitarian rationality (and the scientistic ideologies from which they derive), and much more receptive to the spiritual messages of both our own largely-forgotten tradition and of non-Western cultures alike.

Mark Linenthal has claimed, persuasively enough, that Ginsberg, "more than any other writer changed what a whole generation thought a poem should or could be".[28] Our interest here is not so much in the literary upheaval unleashed by the first public reading of "Howl" (1955) — the "most widely sold, read, and discussed poem of the decade"[29] — but rather in the inter-relationships of aesthetics, politics and metaphysics in Ginsberg's life and work. Clearly the "alteration in consciousness" of which he so often spoke encompasses all of these dimensions. Ginsberg once defined classical poetry as "a 'process', or experiment — a probe into the nature of reality and the nature of the mind".[30] How easily the definition fits Buddhism itself. Ginsberg repeatedly talks of "new consciousness" as providing the emergent Beat writers with their focal point and as impelling their interest in writers such as Blake, Rimbaud, Baudelaire, and Yeats ("our great grandfathers among hermetic poets and philosophers").[31] Of course, since time immemorial poetry has been the medium in which the religious sensibility most readily and fully expresses itself; think of Homer, the Psalms, the rhapsodies of the Vedic rishis.[32] "Poet is Priest", as Ginsberg puts it in the first line of "Death to Van Gogh's Ear".

The Beats' search for new consciousness and for new poetic forms, their rejection of the General Motors/Walt Disney version of the American Dream, their impulse to escape the grip of Urizen (Blake's mythical personification of "Single Vision": instrumentalist rationality, the Human Imagination petrified, Newton's Pantocrator) were all of a piece:

> We didn't have what you would call a philosophy. I would say there was an ethos, that there were ideas...themes... preoccupations...the primary thing was a move towards spiritual liberation, not merely from Bourgeois, 50's quietism, or Silent Generation, but from the last centuries of mechanization and homogenization of cultures, the mechanical assault on human nature and all nature culminating in the bomb...the search for new consciousness...I don't think we had it clearly defined, but we were looking for something...as a kind of breakthrough from the sort of hyper-rationalistic, hyper-scientific, hyper-rationalizing of the post-war era.[33]

As Michael McClure put it in his memoir *Scratching the Beat Surface*, "None of us wanted to go back to the gray, chill, militaristic silence, to the intellective void — to the land without poetry — to the spiritual drabness. We wanted to make it new...We wanted voice and we wanted vision."[34] Here indeed were "angelheaded hipsters burning for ancient heavenly connection"! In this context it is no surprise that a good many of the Beat circle developed a serious and sustained interest in aspects of Eastern religion, art and philosophy — Kerouac, Snyder, Kenneth Rexroth, Philip Whalen, Anne Waldman amongst them.

The whole literary experiment of the Beats, at least for Ginsberg (and certainly for Kerouac and Snyder) was impelled by a spiritual rather than an aesthetic aspiration. Or, to put it differently, the new literary forms emerged out of the explorations of consciousness rather than out of any coherent aesthetic theory, and certainly not out of any blind iconoclasm. As is so often the case with avant-garde movements in whatever domain, theory followed practice. Thus Ginsberg himself succinctly characterized the Beat movement: "a spiritual revolution that took form in the changes in the literary method...".[35] Or again, to put the point differently, poetry, for Ginsberg, became a form of spiritual practice, one nicely attuned to the spiritual economy of Buddhism with its pervasive concern with "the texture of consciousness", underpinned by a metaphysic of "emptiness" or "voidness" (*shūnyatā*) which, far from constituting a nihilistic negation, provided the basis for what Ginsberg called "continuous generous activity, exuberant activity", without hope or fear, non-attached and compassionate; in short, for *karuna*.[36] Ginsberg repeatedly foregrounds the intersections of meditational practice and the writing of poetry: in each case it is a matter of "noticing my thoughts, noticing that I'm noticing it, observing what's there, then realizing what is really there...being a stenographer of your own mind... scanning your mind and observing your thoughts, and what forms arise and flourish".[37] Thus "there's a natural affinity between non-theistic practice and up to date modern and post-modern American poetic practice".[38]

Ginsberg, like other artists and intellectuals who have turned Eastwards, also had a role to play in what Mircea

Eliade has called the "deprovincializing" of Western culture in a "crepuscular era".[39] The epoch of self-contained and more or less homogeneous civilizations is, of course, long since gone. As Lyotard remarked of the "postmodernist" condition, "One listens to reggae, watches a western, eats McDonald's food for lunch and local cuisine for dinner, wears Paris perfume in Tokyo and 'retro' clothes in Hong Kong".[40] He might have added something about mantras, mandalas, mudras or maharishis! The cultural fabric itself becomes a Barthesian text, "a tissue of quotations drawn from the innumerable centers of culture".[41] In Ginsberg's case it was a matter of a disaffiliated American Jew of Russian background careering around America chanting Hindu mantras, reciting Blake and Whitman, playing an Indian harmonium and Aboriginal song sticks, expounding Tibetan metaphysics, quoting Milarepa, Jewish mystics and the Sixth Patriarch.

On one level one might suppose that a good deal of the Beat/counter-cultural infatuation with the exotic, the "oriental", the "mystical" and "magical" was indeed of a sentimental and fashionable order. Doubtless, there was a good deal of counterfeit spirituality peddled by false gurus, by charlatans and hucksters, as there is today under the canopy of New Age-ism. But, no question, the interest in Eastern spirituality met some deep yearning for a vision of reality deeper, richer, more adequate, more attuned to the fullness of human experience, than the impoverished worldview offered by a scientifically-grounded humanism. In short, the Beats and the hippies said "no way José!" to the "grand narrative" of the Enlightenment, and turned to other sources for the wellsprings of wisdom and individual and collective well-being — the religious traditions of the East, the beliefs and practices of indigenous cultures, the quasi-mystical experiences apparently offered by drugs, the mythology and mystical literature enshrined in the pre-Renaissance traditions of the West, and the like.

A serious American engagement with Eastern religions goes back at least to Emerson and Thoreau, and indeed, the Beats counted the Transcendentalists amongst their progenitors.[42] Other obvious precursors include the Theosophists of the late 19th century and the "California Vedantists" (Gerald Heard, Aldous Huxley, Christopher Isherwood and others) of the inter-war period, the latter originating in Vivekananda's influence at the World Parliament of Religions in Chicago in 1893. The Beat and counter-cultural involvement in Eastern spirituality was not without precedent; nor was it either ephemeral or trivial and, indeed, it is still bearing fruit. The adherence of a rapidly growing and highly significant portion of the Western intelligentsia — artists, writers, philosophers, social activists prominently — to Eastern religious forms (most notably from the Tibetan and Japanese branches of Buddhism), and the assimilation of Asian modes of spiritual experience and cultural expression into Western forms, is one of the more remarkable cultural metamorphoses of the late 20th century, one as yet barely recognized let alone understood. More particularly, the impact of the Tibetan diaspora on the West demands more serious attention.

A FEW REFLECTIONS PROVOKED BY THE CURRENT PANDEMIC

S I N C E   T H E 18th century and the so-called Enlightenment the European world, including its extensions in many parts of the globe, has been tyrannized by an outlook which germinated in the Renaissance and the Scientific Revolution of the 17th century, bringing in its wake the destruction of those traditional beliefs and values which had nourished medieval Christendom. This modern worldview — boastfully rationalistic, utilitarian, materialistic, scientistic, technocratic — has by now spread to all parts of the globe. Like a runaway juggernaut, it has obliterated traditional cultures and peoples everywhere, vandalized the natural order and corrupted our very way of seeing and being in the world (this latter diminution being the necessary antecedent of environmental pollution). One of its shibboleths is the idea of "Progress" and its attendant belief that through reason and modern science man can fashion the world to his own ends, seizing his destiny in his own hands. The Enlightenment champions of Progress assured us that a new and better order was at hand (as their epigones are still doing today). The religious beliefs and values vouchsafed by tradition — in contemporary idiom, "the superstitions of the past" — could simply be consigned to the rubbish bin of history. After the blood-stained barbarisms and ecological catastrophes of the 20th century, largely fuelled by an obsessive pursuit of economic "growth", one would hardly have thought that such arrogant and naïve ideas could survive but, in the face of overwhelming evidence to the contrary, they have proved remarkably tenacious. The pandemic, whatever its material and auxiliary causes might be, serves to remind us again that a Promethean hubris must bring consequences in its trail. As Wendell Berry has presciently observed, "Whether we and our politicians know it or not, Nature is party to all our deals and decisions, and she has more votes, a longer memory, and a sterner sense of justice than we do".[1]

Traditional teachings insist that the world and humankind have a divine origin and purpose. Man can only fulfill his vocation by recognizing the Absolute (in Christian terms, God, but elsewhere known by many names) and the imperatives that this entails, including a life of prayer which is our safest refuge and surest hope. Further, we live in a necessarily imperfect world, one in which suffering is inherent; our dealings with each other and with the natural world of which we are a part must be informed by humility, generosity and compassion. Tradition also teaches us that without a sense of the transcendent, a sense of the sacred, no civilization is worth the name. To imagine that the pandemic is unrelated to our willful turning away from these perennial truths is, to say the least, foolish and presumptuous. Neither a "humanism" which answers to nothing outside the human order, nor a profane empirical science, nor a rapacious economic system can provide the remedy for the deep-rooted spiritual crisis of which these are actually both symptom and cause. We cannot too often be reminded that, "The state of the outer world does not merely correspond to the general state of men's souls; it also in some sense depends on that state, since man himself is the pontiff of the outer world. Thus the corruption of man must necessarily affect the whole".[2]

In the circumstances in which we find ourselves we would do well also to heed these words from Frithjof Schuon: "The discomforts or misfortunes which come to man always have three causes — man himself, the world and God. We may, according to the point of view adopted, take into consideration one or other of these causes, but we cannot deny any one of them. Man is the author of his misfortune in so far as it is experienced as suffering; the world is its author in so far as the misfortune seeks to keep man in the cosmic illusion; God is the Author inasmuch as the misfortune comes to man as a sanction, though also as a purification and so as a test".[3] Do we have the wise humility to ask ourselves, in a spirit of severe seriousness, for what transgressions our current sufferings might be a sanction, and to ponder deeply how we might best meet this test and thereby undergo purification, not only of ourselves but of our darkened world? Without an unsparing self-examination of this kind we may, in one way or another, be doomed.

Bendigo, April 2020

NOTES

Religion, the Perennial Philosophy and Traditionalism

1 *Nation Review* was an Australian Sunday newspaper that was launched in 1970 and ceased publication in 1981.
2 Jacob Needleman ed., *The Sword of Gnosis: Metaphysics, Cosmology, Tradition, Symbolism* (Baltimore: Penguin Books, 1974).
3 This was originally published in 1968 under the title *In the Tracks of Buddhism* (London: Allen & Unwin).
4 A set of common metaphysical questions that Buddha refused to answer. Thich Nhat Hanh explains: "The Buddha always told his disciples not to waste their time and energy in metaphysical speculation. Whenever he was asked a metaphysical question, he remained silent. Instead, he directed his disciples toward practical efforts. Questioned one day about the problem of the infinity of the world, the Buddha said, "Whether the world is finite or infinite, limited or unlimited, the problem of your liberation remains the same." Another time he said, "Suppose a man is struck by a poisoned arrow and the doctor wishes to take out the arrow immediately. Suppose the man does not want the arrow removed until he knows who shot it, his age, his parents, and why he shot it. What would happen? If he were to wait until all these questions have been answered, the man might die first." Life is so short. It must not be spent in endless metaphysical speculation that does not bring us any closer to the truth"; from Thich Nhat Hanh & Philip Kapleau, *Zen Keys* (Three Leaves Press, 2005) p. 42; https://encyclopediaofbuddhism.org/wiki/The_unanswered_questions
5 S.H. Nasr, *Ideals and Realities of Islam* (London: Unwin & Allen, 1975), p.15.

Buddhism and the Spiritual Encounter of East and West

1 On this subject and with particular reference to Tibet see Anagarika Govinda, *The Way of the White Clouds* (Boulder: Shambhala, 1970) and Marco Pallis, *The Way and the Mountain* (London: Peter Owen, 1960) These words, written elsewhere by Pallis, are well worth pondering: "One can truly say that this remote land [Tibet] behind the snowy rampart of the Himalaya had become like the chosen sanctuary for

all those things whereof the historical discarding had caused our present profane civilization, the first of its kind, to come into being ... the violation of this sanctuary and the dissipation of the sacred influences concentrated there became an event of properly cosmic significance, of which the ulterior consequences for a world which tacitly condoned the outrage or, in many cases, openly countenanced it on the plea that it brought 'progress' to a reluctant people, have yet to ripen." *Review of The New Religions* by Jacob Needleman in *Studies in Comparative Religion*, 5:3, 1971, pp. 189-190.

2 Frithjof Capra, *The Tao of Physics* (London: Fontana, 1976).

Looking Forward to Tradition

1 René Guénon, *The Reign of Quantity & the Signs of the Times* (first published 1945) (Ghent, NY: Sophia Perennis et Universalis, 1995), pp. 251-252.

2 Frithjof Schuon, *Light on the Ancient Worlds* (Bloomington: World Wisdom, 2006), p. 25.

3 http://www.searchquotes.com/quotes/about/Traditions/

4 Eno and Driver quotes at: http://www.brainyquote.com

5 Krishnamurti and Ellis quotes at: http://www.goodreads.com/quotes/tag/tradition

6 For some comments about these associations see Frithjof Schuon, *Logic and Transcendence* (London: Perennial Books, 1975), p. 6.

7 http://thinkexist.com/quotations/traditions/2.html

8 F.R. Leavis in *Two Cultures* (1962), quoted in Andrew Milner, *Contemporary Cultural Theory* (Sydney: Allen & Unwin, 1991), p. 27.

9 T.S. Eliot, *Selected Prose* (Harmondsworth: Penguin, 1953), p. 20.

10 T.S. Eliot, *Notes towards a Definition of Culture* (London: Faber, 1965), p. 31.

11 Guénon, *The Reign of Quantity*, pp. 251-252.

12 While Ananda Coomaraswamy, the great art historian and savant, occasionally used the term "traditionalist" in a straightforward way to describe an outlook in conformity with traditional principles, Guénon himself applied it negatively to certain individuals who in reaction to the relentless march of modernity were calling for some kind of traditional restoration in the West although they were themselves unaware of the true nature of tradition: "people who," as Guénon wrote, "have only a sort of tendency or aspiration towards tradition without really knowing anything at all about it...". (*Reign of Quantity*, pp. 251-252.) He called these people "traditionalists" and their vague objectives "traditionalism" which he contrasted with "the true traditional spirit". It is important to note in this context that, at that time, a Guénonian school guided by a proper understanding of tradition had not yet emerged, and by the time such a movement began to take shape mid-century, not only were both Guénon and Coomaraswamy no longer alive, but the war years had effectively put an end to such revivalist agitation as Guénon had in mind when he first used those terms. Therefore, some three decades later when

the new traditionalist movement had established itself and attracted sufficient attention, it was inevitable that the term "traditionalism" should be used to describe its message and that its members be called "traditionalists". If the traditionalists themselves have used the term cautiously this is doubtless because they do not see themselves as a "school", nor the principles they affirm as constituting any kind of "-ism". See Schuon, *Logic and Transcendence*, p. 6, and Seyyed Hossein Nasr, *Knowledge and the Sacred* (New York: Crossroad, 1981), p. 104.

13 Coomaraswamy, of English and Sri Lankan parentage, was an art historian, philosopher and Curator of the Asian collection of the Boston Museum of Fine Arts. Schuon was born in Alsace of German parents, trained as a textile designer, spent time in North Africa and eventually became a Sufi Shaykh. He is the author of some thirty books on religious and metaphysical subjects. Titus Burckhardt (1908-1984), a schooldays friend of Schuon, worked in publishing, and was the author of many books on sacred arts and sciences. Marco Pallis (1895-1989) was a musician, mountaineer and the author of several luminous works on Buddhism. Martin Lings (1909-2005) was for many years Keeper of Oriental Manuscripts at the British Museum, a poet, author and spiritual teacher. Seyyed Hossein Nasr (b. 1931) is recognized as one of the leading Islamicists in the contemporary world and holds a chair at George Washington University.

14 Quoted in Sarvepalli Radhakrishnan, "Fragments of a Confession", in *The Philosophy of Sarvepalli Radhakrishnan*, ed. P. A. Schilpp (New York: Tudor, 1952), p. 80.

15 René Guénon in *La Gnose*, 1909, quoted in Whitall Perry, *A Treasury of Traditional Wisdom* (London: Allen & Unwin, 1971), p. 20.

16 See Ananda Coomaraswamy, "Vedanta and Western Tradition" in *Selected Papers 2: Metaphysics*, ed. Roger Lipsey (Princeton: Princeton University Press, 1977), p. 7. See also S.H. Nasr, *Knowledge and the Sacred*, p. 74.

17 Frithjof Schuon, "The Perennial Philosophy", in *The Unanimous Tradition*, ed. Ranjit Fernando (Colombo: Sri Lanka Institute of Traditional Studies, 1991), p. 21. When comparing the terms sophia perennis and philosophia perennis Schuon explains that he prefers "the term sophia to that of philosophia, because the latter is less direct and in addition it evokes associations of ideas with a completely profane and all too often aberrant system of thought". See also Frithjof Schuon, *The Feathered Sun* (Bloomington: World Wisdom, 1990), p. 114, where he refers to this underlying unity or totality as the Primordial *Sanatana Dharma*.

18 *Bhagavad Gita* 4.6.

19 St John 8:58. For a brief commentary see Marco Pallis, *A Buddhist Spectrum* (London: Allen & Unwin, 1980), p. 157.

20 Chou Li: "The true doctrine has always existed in the world" (quoted in W. Perry, *A Treasury of Traditional Wisdom*, p. 794); St Augustine: "That which is called the Christian Religion existed among the Ancients, and never did not exist, from the beginning of the human race" (quoted in S. Radhakrishnan, "Fragments of a Confession", p. 80);

Plotinus: "There must first be one from which the many arise. This one is competent to lend itself to all yet remain one...this is identity in variety" (in W. Perry, *A Treasury of Traditional Wisdom*, p. 776).

21 Ananda Coomaraswamy, *Time and Eternity* (New Delhi: Munshiram Manoharlal, 1993), p. 42n.

22 Coomaraswamy in Letter to Vasudeva Saharan Agrawala, March 1939, *Selected Letters of Ananda Coomaraswamy*, ed. Rama Coomaraswamy & Alvin Moore Jr (New Delhi: Oxford University Press/Indira Gandhi National Center, 1988), p. 168.

23 Pallis cited in the Introduction to R. Fernando, *The Unanimous Tradition*, p. 1.

24 A caution must here be issued against seeing any particular tradition as no more than a temporal continuity of the Primordial Tradition. Guénon's work sometimes leaves the way open for this kind of misunderstanding. For a definitive treatment of the relationship between Tradition and the traditions see Seyyed Hossein Nasr, *Knowledge and the Sacred*, Ch 2, esp. pp. 66-69, 74; See also Whitall Perry, "The Revival of Interest in Tradition" in *The Unanimous Tradition*.

25 Marco Pallis, *The Way and the Mountain* (London: Peter Owen, 1960), p. 203.

26 Brian Keeble, "Tradition, Intelligence and the Artist", *Studies in Comparative Religion*, 11:4, 1977, p. 236. The same point is made in Nasr, *Knowledge and the Sacred*, p. 69.

27 R. Guénon, *The Reign of Quantity*, p. 253.

28 B. Keeble, "Tradition, Intelligence and the Artist", p. 239.

29 M. Pallis, *The Way and the Mountain*, p. 9.

30 T.S. Eliot, *Notes towards a Definition of Culture*, p. 28.

31 Gershon Scholem, "Tradition and Commentary as Religious Categories in Judaism", *Studies in Comparative Religion*, 3:3, 1969, p. 148.

32 W. Perry, "The Revival of Interest in Tradition", p. 3 (emphasis mine).

33 Lord Northbourne, *Religion in the Modern World* (London: Perennial Books/J.M. Dent, 1963), p. 34.

34 A.K. Saran, "The Crisis of Hinduism", *Studies in Comparative Religion*, 5:2, 1971, p. 93.

35 S.H. Nasr, *Knowledge and the Sacred*, p. 68.

36 Frithjof Schuon, *Treasures of Buddhism* (Bloomington: World Wisdom, 1993), p. 8.

37 Frithjof Schuon, *The Transfiguration of Man* (Bloomington: World Wisdom, 1995), p. 18.

38 Frithjof Schuon, *Understanding Islam* (Bloomington: World Wisdom, 1998), p. 26.

39 One of the most eloquent statements of this principle can be found in the Foreword to A. Govinda, *The Way of the White Clouds* (Boulder: Shambhala, 1970), pp. xi-xii. A traditional society will not necessarily be self-consciously aware of being "traditional": the conditions pertaining to a traditional order will appear to be natural and normal, no other possibility having intruded itself.

40 F. Schuon, *The Transfiguration of Man*, p. 28. See also *Treasures of Buddhism*, pp. 13ff; *Light on the Ancient Worlds*, p. 18; and Abu Bakr

Siraj Ed-Din, "The Spiritual Function of Civilization" in *The Sword of Gnosis*, ed, Jacob Needleman (Baltimore: Penguin, 1972), pp. 104ff.

41 R. Guénon, quoted in Roger Lipsey, *Coomaraswamy: Life and Work* (Princeton: Princeton University Press, 1977), p. 266.

42 G.K. Chesterton, *What I Saw in America*, p. 40 (electronic text at: http://books.google.com.au/books).

43 Titus Burckhardt, Alchemy: *Science of the Cosmos, Science of the Soul* (Baltimore: Penguin, 1972), p. 17.

44 Titus Burckhardt, *An Introduction to Sufi Doctrine* (Wellingborough: Thorsons, 1976), p. 17.

45 Schuon has addressed this issue in unequivocal terms: "It is therefore our increasing weakness, and with it the risk of forgetfulness and betrayal, which more than anything obliges us to externalize or make explicit what at the beginning was included in an inward and implicit perfection. Saint Paul needed neither Thomism nor cathedrals, for all profundities and splendors were in himself and all around him in the sanctity of the early community. And this, far from supporting iconoclasts of all kinds, refutes them completely; more or less late epochs — the Middle Ages, for example — have an imperious need for externalizations and developments, just as water from a spring, if it is not to be lost on its way, needs a channel made by nature or by the hand of man; and just as the channel does not transform the water and is not meant to do so — for no water is better than spring water — so the externalizations and developments of a spiritual patrimony are there, not to change that patrimony, but to transmit it as fully and effectively as possible"; Light on the *Ancient Worlds*, p. 5.

46 The term should not here be confused with its more restricted meaning, designating certain artistic and literary developments originating in late 19th century Europe.

47 Lord Northbourne, *Religion in the Modern World*, p. 13.

48 See Seyyed Hossein Nasr, 'Reflections on Islam and Modern Thought', *The Islamic Quarterly* 23:3, 1979, pp. 119-131.

49 Frithjof Schuon, *To Have a Center* (Bloomington: World Wisdom, 1990), p. 37.

50 Blake quoted in Kathleen Raine, 'The Underlying Order: Nature and the Imagination' in *Fragments of Infinity: Essays in Religion and Philosophy*, ed. Arvind Sharma (Bridport: Prism Press, 1991), p. 208.

51 Introduction to *The Oxford Book of Modern Verse* (Oxford: O.U.P., 1936).

52 David Berlinsky, *The Devil's Delusion: Atheism and Its Scientific Pretensions* (New York: Basic Books, 2009), p. 7.

53 D. Berlinsky, *The Devil's Delusion*, p. 16.

54 E.F. Schumacher, *A Guide for the Perplexed* (London: Jonathan Cape, 1977), p. 31.

55 D. Berlinsky, *The Devil's Delusion*, p. 8.

56 Kathleen Raine's image cited in Theodore Roszak, *Where the Wasteland Ends* (New York: Doubleday, 1972), p. 264.

57 F. Schuon, *Light on the Ancient Worlds*, p. 33. See also Schuon, To Have a Center, pp. 11-12.

58 R. Guénon, *L'Erreur Spirite* (1923), quoted in Ananda Coomaraswamy, Hinduism and Buddhism (Delhi: Munshiram Manoharlal, 1996), p. 61.

59 F. Schuon, *Logic and Transcendence* (New York: Harper & Row, 1975), p. 42.

60 In a passage of singular importance, Guénon wrote, "when profane science leaves the domain of a mere observation of facts, and tries to get something out of the indefinite accumulation of separate details which is its sole immediate result, it retains as one of its chief characteristics the more or less laborious construction of purely hypothetical theories. These theories can necessarily never be more than hypothetical, since their starting point is wholly empirical, for facts in themselves are always susceptible of diverse explanations... and besides, such hypotheses are really not inspired by the results of experience to nearly the same extent as by certain preconceived ideas and by some of the predominant tendencies of the modern mentality"; *Reign of Quantity*, p. 149.

61 Frithjof Schuon, "No Activity Without Truth" in *The Sword of Gnosis*, 28. (A different translation of this article can be found in *The Betrayal of Tradition: Essays on the Spiritual Crisis of Modernity*, ed. Harry Oldmeadow [Bloomington: World Wisdom, 2004], pp. 3-14).

62 Frithjof Schuon, "On the Margin of Liturgical Improvisations" in *The Sword of Gnosis*, 353

63 On this subject see Mircea Eliade, "Religious Symbolism and Modern Man's Anxiety" in *Myths, Dreams and Mysteries* (New York: Harper & Row, 1975), pp. 231-245.

64 Schuon, "No Activity Without Truth", p. 39.

65 These are the concluding words of René Guénon's *La Crise du Monde Moderne* (1927). This translation is taken from the *Vincit Omnia Veritas* website: http://www.religioperennis.org/ruh.religioperennis.org/index.html

On Schuon's *Treasures of Buddhism*

1 The book first appeared in English translation as *In the Tracks of Buddhism* (London: Allen & Unwin, 1968). A revised version was published by World Wisdom in 1993. The present volume is a new translation with further revisions. For more details see "Editor's Preface" to the latest edition.

2 William Stoddart, Foreword to Harry Oldmeadow, *Frithjof Schuon and the Perennial Philosophy* (Bloomington: World Wisdom, 2010), p. vii.

3 *In the Tracks of Buddhism*, p. 82. (This passage was omitted from *Treasures of Buddhism*.)

On Marco Pallis' *The Way and the Mountain*

1 Huston Smith quoted by Joseph Fitzgerald in the Introduction to the 2008 edition of *The Way and the Mountain* p.xix. Many other scholars and writers have applauded Pallis' work, among them Gary Snyder, Wendell Berry, Robert Aitken, Joseph Campbell and Thomas Merton.

Five East-West Bridge-builders

1 H. Smith, *Religions of Man* (New York Harper, 1958), p. 355.
2 B. Foxe, *Long Journey Home* (London: Rider, 1975), p. 36.
3 B. Foxe, *Long Journey Home*, p. 17.
4 B. Foxe, *Long Journey Home*, p. 21.
5 "Dutt" in some English renderings.
6 For a brief account of Vivekananda's life and work see W. Halbfass, *India and Europe* (Delhi: Motilal Banarsidass, 1990), pp. 228-246.
7 B. Foxe, *Long Journey Home*, p. 19.
8 C. Isherwood, *Ramakrishna and His Disciples* (Calcutta: Advaita Ashram, 1974), p. 324.
9 B. Foxe, *Long Journey Home*, p. 37.
10 B. Foxe, *Long Journey Home*, p. 92.
11 B. Foxe, *Long Journey Home*, p. 82.
12 See B. Foxe, *Long Journey Home*, pp. 123-124.
13 B. Foxe, *Long Journey Home*, pp. 127-128.
14 B. Foxe, *Long Journey Home*, p. 125. This last reference is to Professor Patrick Geddes, the British sociologist and participant in the Paris Congress of the History of Religions in 1900. Sister Nivedita briefly assisted him with his work.
15 Christine Greenstidel, German by birth, American by citizenship and another of Vivekananda's Western disciples; see her "Memories of Swami Vivekananda" in *Vedanta for the Western World*, ed. C. Isherwood (London: Allen & Unwin, 1963), pp. 156-175.
16 B. Foxe, *Long Journey Home*, p. 166.
17 B. Foxe, *Long Journey Home*, p. 173
18 B. Foxe, *Long Journey Home*, p. 183.
19 B. Foxe, *Long Journey Home*, p. 166.
20 R. Kipling, *Kim* (London: Macmillan, 1927), p. 8.
21 Coomaraswamy quoted in S.K. Abe, "Inside the Wonder House", in *Curators of the Buddha*, ed. D. Lopez Jr. (Chicago: University of Chicago, 1995) p. 81.
22 B. Foxe, *Long Journey Home*, p. 200.
23 B. Foxe, *Long Journey Home*, p. 225.
24 E. Sharpe, *Comparative Religion*, (London: Duckworth, 1975), p. 161.
25 See John Harvey's Translator's Preface to the second edition of *The Idea of the Holy* (Oxford: OUP, 1958), p. xix.
26 N. Söderblom, "Holiness" in *Encyclopedia of Religion and Ethics*, ed. J. Hastings (Edinburgh, T. & T. Clark, 1911), Vol 6, p. 731.
27 R. Otto, *The Idea of the Holy*, p. 7.
28 R. Otto, *The Idea of the Holy*, p. 17
29 R. Otto, *The Idea of the Holy*, Appendix 2.
30 For biographical sketches of Otto see H. Turner & P. Mackenzie, Commentary on *The Idea of the Holy*, (Aberdeen: privately published, undated); Gregory D. Alles in R. Otto, *Autobiographical and Social Essays* (Berlin: Mouton de Gruyter, 1996); P. Almond, *Rudolf Otto* (Chapel Hill: University of North Carolina, 1984).

31 J. Wach, *Types of Religious Experience* (Chicago: University of Chicago, 1951), p. 213.
32 G. Alles in R. Otto, *Autobiographical and Social Essays*, p. 9.
33 G. Alles in R. Otto, *Autobiographical and Social Essays*, p. 9.
34 J. Wach, *Types of Religious Experience*, pp. 210-211.
35 See P. Almond, *Rudolf Otto*, pp. 24-25.
36 From H. Turner & P. Mackenzie, Commentary on *The Idea of the Holy*, 4. For another translation of this passage see R. Otto, *Autobiographical and Social Essays*, p. 80.
37 R. Otto, *Mysticism East and West* (New York: Meridian, 1957), p. v.
38 R. King, *Orientalism and Religion* (London: Routledge, 1999), p. 126.
39 Quoted in P. Almond, *Rudolf Otto*, pp. 23-24. For a similar epiphany experienced by a Western Christian in the face of traditional sculptures see Thomas Merton's moving account of his encounter with the Buddha figures of Polanuwurra in Sri Lanka, in *The Asian Journal of Thomas Merton* (New York: New Directions, 1975), pp. 131-136. See also Henri Le Saux's description of his experience at Elephanta which left him "thunderstruck", in O. Baumer-Despeigne, "The Spiritual Journey of Henri Le Saux-Abhishiktananda", *Cistercian Studies*, 18, 1983, p. 322. See also Bede Griffiths' account of a very similar experience at Elephanta in *The Marriage of East and West* (London: Collins, 1982), pp. 10-11.
40 See H. Rollmann, "Rudolf Otto and India", *Religious Studies Review*, 5:34, July 1979. See Otto's remarks on Gandhi's devotion to the *Gita* in *Autobiographical and Social Essays*, p. 204.
41 R. Otto, *Autobiographical and Social Essays*, p. 203.
42 See P. Almond, "Rudolf Otto and Buddhism" in *Aspects of Religion*, ed. P. Masefield & D. Wiebe (New York: Peter Lang, 1994,) and R. Otto, "Professor Rudolf Otto on Zen", *The Eastern Buddhist* 3:2, Jul-Sept 1924, pp. 117-125.
43 See H. Dumoulin, *Zen Buddhism in the 20th Century* (New York: Weatherhill, 1992), p. 5.
44 R. Otto, *Autobiographical and Social Essays*, 145.
45 G. Alles in R. Otto, *Autobiographical and Social Essays*, p. 11.
46 R. Otto, "Parallelisms in the Development of Religion East and West", *Transactions of the Asiatic Society of Japan*, 40, 1912, 158, quoted in P. Almond "Rudolf Otto and Buddhism", p. 69.
47 M. Eliade, "Giuseppe Tucci", *History of Religions*, 24:2, Nov 1984, p. 57. On Eliade's relationship with Tucci see Gherado Gnoli's obituary, "Mircea Eliade", *East and West*, 36:1-3, Sept 1986, pp. 281-296.
48 E. Conze, *Memoirs of a Modern Gnostic* (Sherbourne: Samzidat, 1979), Vol 2, p. 51; for reflections on Tucci see pp. 47-53.
49 For a brief account of Tucci's career see L. Petech, "Giuseppe Tucci", *Journal of the International Association for Buddhist Studies*, 7, 1984, pp. 137-142.
50 G. Tucci, Tibet, *Land of Snows* (London: Paul Elek, 1967), pp. 13-14.
51 G. Tucci, "A Propos East and West", *East and West*, 8, 1958, p. 346.
52 For some discussion of the medieval theme in Mariani and others see P. Bishop, *The Myth of Shangri-La*, London, 1989.
53 G. Tucci, *To Lhasa and Beyond* (Ithaca: Snow Lion, 1983), p. 8.

54 For Tucci's comments on Tenzing see *Tibet, Land of Snows*, p. 13.
55 T. Norgay, *Man of Everest* (London: Harrap, 1955), pp. 112-114.
56 Preface to *To Lhasa and Beyond*, 1983 ed., p. 5.
57 L. Petech, "Giuseppe Tucci", p. 138.
58 Mircea Eliade dedicated *Occultism, Witchcraft and Cultural Fashions* (Chicago: University of Chicago, 1976) to Tucci "in memory of our discussions in Calcutta, 1929-1931".
59 See J. Nattier, "Buddhist Studies in the Post-Colonial Era", *Journal of the American Academy of Religion*, 1997, p. 476.
60 S. Batchelor, *The Awakening of the West* (Berkeley: Parallax, 1994), p. 317.
61 See T. Norgay, *Man of Everest*, pp. 119-120.
62 L. Petech, "Giuseppe Tucci", p. 139.
63 M. Eliade, "Giuseppe Tucci", p. 158n.
64 See D. Lopez, *Prisoners of Shangri-La* (Chicago: University of Chicago, 1998), p. 353n.
65 G. Tucci, *The Theory and Practice of the Mandala* (London: Rider, 1961), p. viii.
66 G. Tucci, "A Propos East and West", pp. 343-4. (Tucci goes on to argue that the difference between Latins and Anglo-Saxons might be as significant as that between Latins and Asians.)
67 A. Watts, *In My Own Way* (New York: Vintage, 1972), p. 439.
68 See P. B. Chowka, "The East West Interview" (April 1977), reproduced in G. Snyder, *The Real Work* (New York: New Directions, 1980, pp. 92-137. (Of the many interviews Snyder has given over the years the East West one with Barry Chowka remains one of the most illuminating.)
69 Snyder quoted in C. Tonkinson (ed), *Big Sky Mind* (New York: Riverhead, 1995), p. 172.
70 For some comments by Snyder on the Roshi see P.B. Chowka, "The East West Interview", pp. 97-98. Other Western students of the Roshi included Janwillem van der Wetering and Irmgard Schloegl—see "Some Further Angles" in *The Real Work*, p. 178.
71 R. Fields, *How the Swans Came to the Lake* (Boston: Shambhala, 1992), pp. 220-221.
72 It is interesting to compare Ginsberg and Snyder's respective accounts of their trip in *Indian Journals March 1962-May 1963* (San Francisco: Dave Haselwood and City Lights, 1970, and *Passage Through India* (San Francisco: Grey Fox, 1983).
73 R. Fields, *How the Swans Came to the Lake*, pp. 294-295.
74 G. Snyder, *Passage Through India*, p. x.
75 R. Fields, *How the Swans Came to the Lake*, p. 248.
76 J.J. Clarke, *Oriental Enlightenment* (London: Routledge, 1997), p. 104.
77 C. Trevor, "The Wild Mind of Gary Snyder", *Shambhala Sun* (website).
78 G. Snyder, *A Place in Space* (Washington DC: Counterpoint, 1995), p. 246.
79 For Snyder's recent ruminations on the Beats, poetry, Zen, Amerindian tradition, ecology and aesthetics, see *A Place in Space*.
80 S. McLean, Introduction to G. Snyder, *The Real Work*, p. xiii.
81 C. Trevor, "The Wild Mind of Gary Snyder", *Shambhala Sun* (website).
82 I came across this quote on a website that has since disappeared.

83 C. Trevor, "The Wild Mind of Gary Snyder", *Shambhala Sun* (website).

84 J. Dodge, Foreword to G. Snyder, *The Gary Snyder Reader* (Washington DC: Counterpoint, 1999), p. xix.

85 The change of title and the addition of the sub-title are both suggestive, as is the insertion of a new segment on primal traditions.

86 H. Smith, *Religions of Man*, p. 11.

87 For biographical details see "Biographical Sketch" in A. Sharma (ed), *Fragments of Infinity* (Bridport: Prism, 1991), pp. xi-xii; M.D. Bryant in H. Smith, *Essays on World Religion* (New York: Paragon House, 1992); H. Smith, *Why Religion Matters* (San Francisco: Harper 2002), pp. xiii-xiv; H. Smith & D.R. Griffin, *Primordial Truth and Postmodern Theology* (Albany: SUNY, 1989).

88 P. Novak, "The Chun-Tzu" in A. Sharma (ed), *Fragments of Infinity*, p. 8.

89 See S.H. Nasr, "Homage to Huston Smith", *Sophia: The Journal of Traditional Studies*, 3:2, Winter 1997, pp. 5-8.

90 Arvind Sharma in A. Sharma (ed), *Fragments of Infinity*, pp. xi-xii.

91 Huston Smith in H. Smith & D.R. Griffin, *Primordial Truth and Postmodern Theology*, p. 13.

92 For details of these and other works see M. Darrol Bryant's Bibliography in H. Smith, *Essays on World Religion*, pp. 286-287. Smith was also gracious enough to write the Foreword for the book from which this article is excerpted, *Journeys East: 20th Century Western Encounters with Eastern Religious Traditions*.

93 A *Newsweek* reviewer of "The Wisdom of Faith with Huston Smith" trivialized Smith as a "spiritual surfer", just as his more academic critics have mistakenly accused him of "eclecticism" and "syncretism". See S. Glazer, *The Heart of Learning* (New York: Putnam, 1999), p. 228, and S.H. Nasr, "Homage to Huston Smith", p. 7.

94 H. Smith, *The World's Religions*, p. 390.

95 M. Gustin, "Tribute to Huston Smith", in A. Sharma (ed), *Fragments of Infinity*, p. 13. For a more recent and more detailed tribute see Harry Oldmeadow, "Huston Smith, Bridge-Builder Extraordinaire: A Tribute", *Sophia: The Journal of Traditional Studies*, 10:1, 2010, pp. 73-80.

Notes on "Spirituality"

1 F. Schuon: "No Activity Without Truth" in Harry Oldmeadow (ed), *The Betrayal of Tradition* (Bloomington: World Wisdom, 2005), p.

2 Barry McDonald (ed), *Every Branch in Me: Essays on the Meaning of Man* (Bloomington: World Wisdom, 2003), p.ix

3 On the disastrous conflation of the psychic and the spiritual see René Guénon, *The Reign of Quantity and the Signs of the Times* (Ghent: Sophia Perennis et Universalis, 1995).

4 Martin Buber, *A Believing Humanism* (New York: Simon & Schuster, 1967), p. 110.

5 Thomas Keating, "Meditative Technologies: Theological Ecumenism" in *The Other Half of My Soul: Bede Griffiths and the Hindu-Christian Dialogue*, ed. Beatrice Bruteau (Wheaton: Quest Books, 1996), p. 115.

6 Kenneth ("Harry") Oldmeadow, *Traditionalism: Religion in the light of the Perennial Philosophy* (Colombo: Sri Lanka Institute of Traditional Studies, 2000), p. 122.
7 Frithjof Schuon, *Stations of Wisdom* (London: John Murray/Perennial, 1961), p. 57.
8 See T.M.P. Mahadevan, *Ramana Maharshi: The Sage of Arunachala* (London: Allen & Unwin, 1977).

Notes on Cosmic Cycles and the Kali Yuga

1 Frithjof Schuon, *The Transcendent Unity of Religions* (Wheaton: Quest, 1993), p. xxxiii.
2 Frithjof Schuon, *Gnosis: Divine Wisdom* (Bloomington: World Wisdom, 2006), p. 45.
3 René Guénon, *Crisis of the Modern World* (London: Luzac, 1975), p. 1.
4 See René Guénon, *The Reign of Quantity and Signs of the Times* (Ghent, NY: Sophia Perennis et Universalis, 1995), pp. 11-12.
5 Frithjof Schuon, *Esoterism as Principle and as Way* (London: Perennial, 1981), p. 162.
6 Frithjof Schuon, *The Feathered Sun* (Bloomington: World Wisdom, 1990) p. 107.
7 Readers interested in more material on the doctrine of cycles and non traditional understandings of time are directed to the following sources: R. Guénon, *Crisis of the Modern World* and *The Reign of Quantity*; A.K. Coomaraswamy, *Time and Eternity* (Ascona: Artibus Asiae, 1947); M. Lings, *Ancient Beliefs and Modern Superstitions* (London: Allen & Unwin, 1980) and *The Eleventh Hour* (Cambridge: Quinta Essentia, 1987); A. Snodgrass, *Architecture, Time and Eternity* (New Delhi: P.K. Goel/Aditya Prakashan, 1990). Interesting commentaries are also to be found in W. Quinn, *The Only Tradition* (Albany: SUNY, 1997); Joseph Campbell (ed), *Man and Time: Papers from the Eranos Yearbooks* (Princeton: Bollingen Series, 1973); Mircea Eliade, *The Myth of the Eternal Return*, and "Religious Symbolism and Modern Man's Anxiety" in *Myths, Dreams and Mysteries* (Chicago: Harper & Row, 1960).
8 See René Guénon, *The Reign of Quantity*, p. 2.
9 Nrsimhacarana Panda, *Cyclic Universe* (New Delhi: D.K. Printworld, 2002), p. 742.
10 The Prophet quoted in William Stoddart, *Remembering in a World of Forgetting* (Bloomington: World Wisdom, 2008), p. 5.
11 Frithjof Schuon, *From the Divine to the Human* (Bloomington: World Wisdom, 1982), p. 98n.
12 Titus Burckhardt, "Cosmology and Modern Science" in *The Sword of Gnosis*, ed. Jacob Needleman (Baltimore: Penguin, 1974), pp. 148-149.
13 Frithjof Schuon, *Gnosis: Divine Wisdom*, p. 45.
14 René Guénon, *Crisis of the Modern World*, p. 1.
15 Frithjof Schuon, *The Feathered Sun*, pp. 113-114.
16 The Vishnu Purana, quoted in William Stoddart, *An Outline of Hinduism* (Washington DC: Foundation for Traditional Studies, 1993),

pp. 75-76. These passages, in a different translation, can be found in *The Vishnu Purana*, Vol 2, tr. & ed. H.H. Wilson & Nag Sharan Singh, (Delhi: Nag Publishers, 1980), pp. 662-3, 866-867.

17 René Guénon, *Traditional Forms and Cosmic Cycles* (Ghent: Sophia Perennis et Universalis, 2001), p. 8.

18 2 Timothy 3:1-7; W. Stoddart, *Remembering in a World of Forgetting*, 64.

19 Frithjof Schuon, *Esoterism as Principle and as Way*, p. 162n.

20 Emil Cioran, *Anathemas and Admirations* (New York: Arcade, 1991), 122.

21 Mircea Eliade, 'Time and Eternity in Indian Thought' in *Man and Time: Papers from the Eranos Yearbooks*, quoted in William Quinn, *The Only Tradition*, p. 123.

22 Aquinas quoted in W. Quinn, *The Only Tradition*, p. 123.

23 See Eliade's fascinating essay on this subject in *Myths, Dreams and Mysteries*.

24 Frithjof Schuon, *Gnosis: Divine Wisdom*, p. 50.

25 Frithjof Schuon, *The Transcendent Unity of Religions*, p. xxxi.

26 Frithjof Schuon, *The Transcendent Unity of Religions*, p. xxxi.

27 Frithjof Schuon, *The Transfiguration of Man* (Bloomington: World Wisdom, 1995), p. 10.

28 Frithjof Schuon, *The Transfiguration of Man*, p. 10.

29 Frithjof Schuon, *Esoterism as Principle and as Way*, p. 19.

30 Frithjof Schuon, *The Transcendent Unity of Religions*, p. xxxi.

31 Frithjof Schuon, *The Transcendent Unity of Religions*, p. xxxi.

32 Frithjof Schuon, *Gnosis: Divine Wisdom*, p. 12. See also W. Perry, *A Treasury of Traditional Wisdom* (London: Allen & Unwin, 1971, p. 22n.

33 Joseph Epes Brown *The Sacred Pipe* (Norman: University of Oklahoma, 1953), p. xii. (This passage was omitted from the later Penguin edition.) See also Schuon's "Human Premises of a Religious Dilemma" in *Sufism: Veil and Quintessence* (Bloomington: World Wisdom, 2007), pp. 97-113.

34 Frithjof Schuon, "No Activity Without Truth" in *The Sword of Gnosis*, p. 39.

35 Frithjof Schuon, "On the Margin of Liturgical Improvisations" in *The Sword of Gnosis*, p. 353.

36 Romans 10:13; W. Stoddart, *Remembering in a World of Forgetting*, 122.

To a Buddhist Beat: Allen Ginsberg on Politics, Poetics and Spirituality

1 Interview with Henry Tischler, "Allen Ginsberg—Journals Mid-Fifties: 1954-1958", http://www.authorsspeak.com/ginsberg [all subsequent Website references are http://www].

2 Susan Sontag, "The Aesthetics of Silence" in *A Susan Sontag Reader*, ed. E. Hardwick (Harmondsworth: Penguin, 1983), p. 181.

3 See Barry Miles, *Ginsberg: A Biography* (New York: Harper Perennial, 1989), p. 446.

4 As well as the Miles biography already cited there is Michael Schumacher's *Dharma Lion: A Critical Biography of Allen Ginsberg* (New York: St. Martin's Press, 1992). For a detailed list of critical and

biographical work on Ginsberg see "Writings about Allen Ginsberg", www.charm.net/~brooklyn/Biblio/GinsbergBiblio.html.

5 Allen Ginsberg, "The Vomit of a Mad Tyger", *Shambhala Sun*, July 1995, shambhalasun.com/ginsberg.html (this source hereafter "Tyger")

6 B. Miles, Ginsberg, p. 99. The most detailed account of this experience is to be found in Ginsberg's interview with Tom Clark in *Paris Review* 37, Spring 1966.

7 Ginsberg, quoted in Theodore Roszak, *The Making of a Counter Culture* (London: Faber, 1969), p. 127.

8 B. Miles, *Ginsberg*, p. 104.

9 Allen Ginsberg, excerpt from *Disembodied Poetics: Annals of the Jack Kerouac School*, naropa.edu/ginsbuddhist2.html. Kerouac himself had first turned to these texts in reaction against Neal Cassady's preoccupation with Edgar Cayce (whom Ginsberg later described as a "crackpot").

10 "Tyger"

11 B. Miles, *Ginsberg*, p. 153.

12 For Ginsberg's account of his experiences in India see *Indian Journals, March 1962-May 1963* (San Francisco: City Lights Books & Dave Haselwood Books, 1970). See also B. Miles, Ginsberg, Chapter 11.

13 For a detailed narrative of Trungpa's part in the spread of Buddhism in America see Rick Fields, *How the Swans Came to the Lake: A Narrative History of Buddhism in America* (Boston: Shambhala, 1992 rev. edit.). For Trungpa's own story of his early life see *Born in Tibet* (Shambhala: Boston, 1995—first published 1966).

14 Canadian Broadcasting Corporation, "Interview with Allen Ginsberg", myna.com/~davidck/giinsb~1.htm

15 Allen Ginsberg, "Meditation and Poetics" in Spiritual Quests: *The Art and Craft of Religious Writing*, ed. William Zinsser (Boston: Houghton Mifflin, 1988), p. 163.

16 Peter Barry Chowka, "This is Allen Ginsberg?", the 1976 *New Age* Interview, members.aol.com/pbchowka/ginsberg76.html

17 "Allen Ginsberg: Anxious Dreams of Eliot", *The Boston Book Review* Interview with Harvey Blume, 1995, www.bookwire.com/bbr/interviews/v2.7/ginsberg.html

18 See "Tyger".

19 See B. Miles, *Ginsberg*, pp. 466-482.

20 See Jack Kornfield, "Is Buddhism Changing in North America?" in *Buddhist America*, ed. Don Morreale (Sante Fe: John Muir Publications, 1988).

21 See Fred Eppsteiner ed., *The Path of Compassion: Writings on Socially Engaged Buddhism* (Berkeley: Parallax Press, 1988).

22 For information about tributes, ceremonies, remembrances and the like, see: tricycle.com/ginsberg.html

23 See Seth Goddard, "The Beats and Boom: A Conversation with Allen Ginsberg", pathfinder.com/@@kPiSQwQAOXm@6@3B/Life/boomers/ginsberg.html

24 "Allen Ginsberg interviewed by Jeffrey Goldsmith" (emphasis mine).

25 "Allen Ginsberg interviewed by Jeffrey Goldsmith".

26 Theodore Roszak, *The Making of a Counter Culture*, p. 141.

27 *The Making of the Counter Culture*, p. 129.

28 "San Francisco Says Goodbye to a Bard", *San Francisco Chronicle*, Monday April 21, 1997, p. A1.

29 Daniel Hoffman ed., *Harvard Guide to Contemporary American Writing* (Cambridge, Massachusetts: The Belknap Press, 1979), p. 519.

30 Allen Ginsberg, "Meditation and Poetics", p. 145.

31 "Meditation and Poetics", p. 148.

32 On this subject see Bede Griffiths, *The Marriage of East and West* (London: Collins, 1982), pp. 47ff.

33 Seth Goddard, "The Beats and Boom: A Conversation with Allen Ginsberg" (italics mine). See also "Allen Ginsberg interviewed by Jeffrey Goldsmith" where Ginsberg says, "My own idea is that the origins of beat writings were in some kind of spiritual revolution."

34 Steve Silberman, "How Beat Happened", ezone.org:1080/ez/e2/articles/digaman.html

35 Seth Goddard, "The Beats and Boom: A Conversation with Allen Ginsberg".

36 "The Beats and Boom".

37 Jim Moore, "Public Heart: An Interview with Allen Ginsberg", bookwire.com/hmr/REVIEW/moore.html

38 Canadian Broadcasting Corporation, "Interview with Allen Ginsberg".

39 See Mircea Eliade, *Autobiography II: 1937-1960, Exile's Odyssey* (Chicago: University of Chicago Press, 1988), pp. 152-153, and *The Quest: History and Meaning in Religion* (Chicago: University of Chicago Press, 1969), pp. 62-63.

40 Jean-François Lyotard quoted in Todd Gitlin, "Style for style's sake" in *The Weekend Australian* January 21-22, 1989, Weekender p. 9.

41 Roland Barthes, "The Death of the Author" in *Image Music Text*, selected and trans. Stephen Heath (London: Fontana, 1977), p. 146.

42 See Rick Fields, *How the Swans Came to the Lake: A Narrative History of Buddhism in America*, Chapter 4, pp. 54-69.

A Few Reflections Provoked by the Current Pandemic

1 From Wendell Berry's endorsement for the book *The Dying of the Trees*, by Charles Little, 1997.

2 Abu Bakr Siraj Ed-Din, 1974, *The Book of Certainty* (New York: Samuel Weiser, 1974), p. 33.

3 Frithjof Schuon, *Spiritual Perspectives and Human Facts* (London: Perennial, 1969), pp. 129-130.

SELECT BIBLIOGRAPHY OF PRINCIPAL SOURCES

Abu Bakr Siraj Ed-Din. 1974, *The Book of Certainty* (New York: Samuel Weiser, 1974).

Almond, Philip. *Rudolf Otto* (Chapel Hill: University of North Carolina, 1984).

Batchelor, Stephen. *The Awakening of the West* (Berkeley: Parallax, 1994).

Berlinsky, David. *The Devil's Delusion: Atheism and Its Scientific Pretensions* (New York: Basic books, 2009).

Burckhardt, Titus. "Cosmology and Modern Science" in *The Sword of Gnosis*, ed. Jacob Needleman (Baltimore: Penguin, 1974).

Campbell, Joseph (ed). *Man and Time: Papers from the Eranos Yearbooks* (Princeton: Bollingen Series, 1973).

Coomaraswamy, Ananda. *Time and Eternity* (Ascona: Artibus Asiae, 1947).

—. *Selected Papers 2: Metaphysics*, ed. Roger Lipsey (Princeton: Princeton University Press, 1977).

—. *Hinduism and Buddhism* (Delhi: Munshiram Manoharlal, 1996).

Desjardins, Arnaud. *The Message of the Tibetans* (London: Stuart & Watkins, 1969).

Eliade, Mircea. *Myths, Dreams and Mysteries* (New York: Harper & Row, 1960).

—. *Occultism, Witchcraft and Cultural Fashions* (Chicago: University of Chicago, 1976).

—. "Time and Eternity in Indian Thought" in *Man and Time: Papers from the Eranos Yearbooks*, ed. Joseph Campbell (Princeton: Bollingen Series, 1983).

Eliot, T.S. *Notes towards the Definition of Culture* (London: Faber, 1969).

Eppsteiner, Fred (ed). *The Path of Compassion: Writings on Socially Engaged Buddhism* (Berkeley: Parallax Press, 1988).

Griffiths, Bede, *The Marriage of East and West* (London: Collins, 1982).

Fernando, Ranjit (ed). *The Unanimous Tradition* (Colombo: Sri Lanka Institute of Traditional Studies, 1991).

Fields, Rick. *How the Swans Came to the Lake* (Boston: Shambhala, 1992).

Foxe, Barbara. *Long Journey Home* (London: Rider, 1975).

Ginsberg, Allen. *Indian Journals March 1962-May 1963* (San Francisco: Dave Haselwood and City Lights, 1970).

—. "Meditation and Poetics" in *Spiritual Quests: The Art and Craft of Religious Writing*, ed. William Zinsser (Boston: Houghton Mifflin, 1988).

—. "The Vomit of a Mad Tyger", *Shambhala Sun*, July 1995, shambhalasun.com/ginsberg.html.

Govinda, Anagarika, *The Way of the White Clouds* (Boulder: Shambhala, 1970).

Guénon, René. *Crisis of the Modern World* (London: Luzac, 1975).

— *The Reign of Quantity and Signs of the Times* (Ghent, NY: Sophia Perennis et Universalis, 1995).

— *Traditional Forms and Cosmic Cycles* (Ghent: Sophia Perennis et Universalis, 2001).

Gustin, Marilyn. "Tribute to Huston Smith", in *Fragments of Infinity*, ed. Arvind Sharma, (Bridport: Prism, 1991).

Halbfass, Wilhelm. *India and Europe* (Delhi: Motilal Banarsidass, 1990).

Isherwood, Christopher. *Ramakrishna and His Disciples* (Calcutta: Advaita Ashram, 1974).

— (ed). Vedanta for the Western World (London: Allen & Unwin, 1963).

Keating, Thomas. "Meditative Technologies: Theological Ecumenism" in *The Other Half of My Soul: Bede Griffiths and the Hindu-Christian Dialogue*, ed. Beatrice Bruteau (Wheaton: Quest Books, 1996).

Lings, Martin. *Ancient Beliefs and Modern Superstitions* (London: Allen & Unwin, 1980).

— *The Eleventh Hour* (Cambridge: Quinta Essentia, 1987).

— & Clinton Minnaar (eds). *The Underlying Religion* (Bloomington: World Wisdom, 2007).

Lopez Jr, Donald. *Prisoners of Shangri-La* (Chicago: University of Chicago, 1998).

— (ed). *Curators of the Buddha* (Chicago: University of Chicago, 1995).

Mahadevan, T.M.P. *Ramana Maharshi: The Sage of Arunachala* (London: Allen & Unwin, 1977).

McDonald, Barry (ed). *Every Branch in Me: Essays on the Meaning of Man* (Bloomington: World Wisdom, 2003).

Merton, Thomas, *The Asian Journal of Thomas Merton*, ed. Naomi Burton et al. (New York: New Directions, 1975).

Miles, Barry. *Ginsberg: A Biography* (New York: Harper Perennial, 1989).

Morreale, Don (ed). *Buddhist America* (Santa Fe: John Muir Publications, 1988).

Nasr, Seyyed Hossein. *Ideals and Realities of Islam* (London: Unwin & Allen, 1975).

—. *Knowledge and the Sacred* (New York: Crossroad, 1981).

—. "Homage to Huston Smith", Sophia, 3:2, Winter 1997.

Needleman, Jacob (ed). *The Sword of Gnosis: Metaphysics, Cosmology, Tradition, Symbolism* (Baltimore: Penguin Books, 1974).

Northbourne, Lord. *Looking Back on Progress* (London: Perennial Books, 1970).

Oldmeadow, Kenneth (Harry). *Traditionalism: Religion in the light of the Perennial Philosophy* (Colombo: Sri Lanka Institute of Traditional Studies, 2000).

Oldmeadow, Harry, *Journeys East: 20th Century Western Encounters with Eastern Religious Traditions* (Bloomington: World Wisdom, 2004).

—. *Frithjof Schuon and the Perennial Philosophy* (Bloomington: World Wisdom, 2010).

—. "Huston Smith, Bridge-Builder *Extraordinaire*: A Tribute", *Sophia: The Journal of Traditional Studies*, 10:1, 2010.

— (ed). *The Betrayal of Tradition* (Bloomington: World Wisdom, 2005).

— (ed). *Light from the East: Eastern Wisdom for the Modern West* (Bloomington: World Wisdom, 2007).

Otto, Rudolf. *The Idea of the Holy* (Oxford: OUP, 1958).

—. *Autobiographical and Social Essays*, ed. Gregory D. Alles (Berlin: Mouton de Gruyter, 1996).

—. *Mysticism East and West* (New York: Meridian, 1957).

Pallis, Marco. *The Way and the Mountain* (London: Peter Owen, 1960; Bloomington: World Wisdom, 2008).

Panda, Nrsimhacarana. *Cyclic Universe* (New Delhi: D.K. Printworld, 2002).

Perry, Whitall. *A Treasury of Traditional Wisdom* (London: Allen & Unwin, 1971).

Quinn, William. *The Only Tradition* (Albany: SUNY, 1997).

Roszak, Theodore. *The Making of a Counter Culture* (London: Faber, 1969).

Schuon, Frithjof. *Stations of Wisdom* (London: John Murray/ Perennial, 1961).

—. *In the Tracks of Buddhism* (London: Allen & Unwin, 1968).

—. *Spiritual Perspectives and Human Facts* (London: Perennial, 1969).

—. *Light on the Ancient Worlds* (Bloomington: World Wisdom, 2006).

—. *Logic and Transcendence* (London: Perennial Books, 1975).

—. *Esoterism as Principle and as Way* (London: Perennial, 1981).

—. *From the Divine to the Human* (Bloomington: World Wisdom, 1982).

—. *The Feathered Sun* (Bloomington: World Wisdom, 1990).

—. *The Transcendent Unity of Religions* (Wheaton: Quest, 1993).

—. *The Transfiguration of Man* (Bloomington: World Wisdom, 1995).

—. *Gnosis: Divine Wisdom* (Bloomington: World Wisdom, 2006).

—. *Sufism: Veil and Quintessence* (Bloomington: World Wisdom, 2007).

—. "No Activity Without Truth" in *The Betrayal of Tradition*, ed. Harry Oldmeadow (Bloomington: World Wisdom, 2005) Also in *The Sword of Gnosis*, ed. Jacob Needleman..

Sharma, Arvind (ed). *Fragments of Infinity* (Bridport: Prism, 1991).

Sharpe, Eric. *Comparative Religion*, (London: Duckworth, 1975).

Smith, Huston. *The Religions of Man* (New York Harper, 1958).

—. *Essays on World Religion* (New York: Paragon House, 1992).

—. *Why Religion Matters* (San Francisco: Harper 2002).

Smith, Huston & D.R. Griffin, *Primordial Truth and Postmodern Theology* (Albany: SUNY 1989).

Snodgrass, Adrian. Architecture, *Time and Eternity* (New Delhi: P.K. Goel/Aditya Prakashan, 1990).

Snyder, Gary. *Passage Through India* (San Francisco: Grey Fox, 1983).

—. *A Place in Space* (Washington DC: Counterpoint, 1995).

—. *The Gary Snyder Reader* (Washington DC: Counterpoint, 1999).

Stoddart, William. *Remembering in a World of Forgetting* (Bloomington: World Wisdom, 2008).

Tonkinson, Carole (ed). *Big Sky Mind* (New York: Riverhead, 1995).

Trungpa, Chogyäm. *Born in Tibet* (Shambhala: Boston, 1995; first published 1966).

Tucci, Giuseppe. *The Theory and Practice of the Mandala* (London: Rider, 1961).

—. *Tibet, Land of Snows* (London: Paul Elek, 1967).

—. *To Lhasa and Beyond* (Ithaca: Snow Lion, 1983).

Wach, Joachim. *Types of Religious Experience* (Chicago: University of Chicago, 1951).

APPENDIX: THE PERENNIALIST SCHOOL

(A) KEY FIGURES

Dates, primary interests, recommended reading.

The works mentioned are suggested starting points for readers coming to these writers for the first time. Two anthologies of traditionalist writings are also strongly recommended: *The Sword of Gnosis*, ed. Jacob Needleman, and *The Underlying Religion*, ed. Martin Lings and Clinton Minnaar.

More biographical and bibliographical details can be found at http://www.worldwisdom.com/public/authors/default. aspx?Display=Authors

Joseph Epes Brown (1920-2000) The cosmology and rites of the Plains Indians of North America. *The Sacred Pipe* and *The Spiritual Legacy of the American Indians*.

Titus Burckhardt (1908-1984) Traditional sciences and cosmology; alchemy; sacred art; Sufism. *Sacred Art East and West* and *Alchemy: Science of the Cosmos, Science of the Soul*.

Ananda Coomaraswamy (1877-1947) Sacred art of Asia; Hinduism and Buddhism; classical, medieval and Indian metaphysics. *Christian and Oriental Philosophy of Art* and *The Bugbear of Literacy*.

René Guénon (1886-1951) (The seminal figure of traditionalism.) Metaphysics, esoterism and initiation; cosmology and symbolism; the critique of modernity. *The Crisis of the Modern World* and *The Reign of Quantity.*

Martin Lings (1909-2005) Islam, Sufism; religion in the modern world. *Ancient Beliefs and Modern Superstitions* and *What is Sufism?*

Seyyed Hossein Nasr (1933-) All aspects of Islamic civilization; science, philosophy and metaphysics; the environmental crisis. *Ideals and Realities of Islam* and *Knowledge and the Sacred.*

Lord Northbourne (1896-1982) Work, agriculture, the natural order. *Religion in the Modern World* and *Of the Land and the Spirit.*

Marco Pallis (1895-1990) (The leading Buddhist perennialist.) All aspects of traditional Tibet. *Peaks and Lamas, The Way and the Mountain* and *A Buddhist Spectrum.*

Whitall Perry (1920-2005) Religion and its counterfeits in the modern world; the manifold expressions of the perennial philosophy in the world's great traditions. *A Treasury of Traditional Wisdom* (edited) and *Challenges to a Secular Society.*

Frithjof Schuon (1907-1998) (The pre-eminent exponent of perennialism.) The perennial philosophy in all its aspects; primordial traditions; sacred art; exoterism and esoterism in the religions, particularly Christianity, Islam and Hinduism. *The Transcendent Unity of Religions* and *Spiritual Perspectives and Human Facts.*

Leo Schaya (1916-1985) Judaism and Kabbalah. *Universal Aspects of the Kabbalah and Judaism.*

Other traditionalists, mainly from the following generation, include Mateus Soares de Azevedo, William Chittick, Jean Cooper, Rama Coomaraswamy, James Cutsinger, Maria Massi Dakake, Gai Eaton, Joseph Fitzgerald, Michael Fitzgerald, Gray Henry, John Herlily, Brian Keeble, Ali Lakhani, Jean-Pierre Lafouge, Patrick Laude, Jean-Louis Michon, Clinton Minnaar, Mark Perry, Reza Shah-Kazemi, Philip Sherrard, Wolfgang Smith, Samuel Bendeck Sotillos, William Stoddart, Charles Upton, and Algis Uždavinys.

The principal forum for contemporary perennialist discourse is *Sacred Web: A Journal of Tradition and Modernity*, based in Vancouver and edited by Ali Lakhani.

(B) GLOSSARY OF TERMS USED IN PERENNIALIST WRITINGS

Esoteric: concerning the inner and universal meanings of religious forms.

Exoteric: concerning outward and visible religious forms.

Intellect (from the Latin *Intellectus*): the inherent, unconditioned, supra-mental faculty by which the Absolute may be directly apprehended; "that which participates in the divine Subject"; hence Intellection refers to this apprehension. (The Greek term for this receptive faculty is nous.)

Gnosis (Greek): "knowledge"; spiritual insight, principial comprehension, divine wisdom.

Logos (Greek): "word, reason"; in Christian theology, the divine, uncreated Word of God; the transcendent Principle of creation and revelation.

Metaphysics: the Science of the Real, of the Absolute and the relative; "concerning universal realities considered objectively" (Schuon).

Mysticism: concerning the soul's experience of supra-phenomenal realities; concerning universal realities considered subjectively.

Orthodox: "the principle of formal homogeneity proper to any authentically spiritual perspective" (Schuon).

Revelation: an "eruption" of the Divine, the Absolute, into the world of time and space, such as issues forth a new "dispensation", a new religious tradition.

Sophia (Greek): "wisdom"; in Jewish and Christian tradition, the Wisdom of God, often conceived as feminine.

Sophia Perennis (Greek): "Perennial Wisdom"; the eternal, non-formal Truth at the heart of all orthodox religious traditions.

Spirit (from the Latin *Spiritus*): the supra-individual principle of the human microcosm, seated in the heart.

Symbol: a reality of a lower order which participates analogically in the reality of a higher order of being.

Tradition: may be used in several related senses: a timeless and universal wisdom of supra-human origin which informs all integral mythologies and religions; an ensemble of religious forms issuing from a Divine Revelation (thus we may speak of "traditions", usually used synonymously with "religions"); the transmission of these forms through time. "Tradition" may also refer to a whole culture which everywhere bears the imprint of the religion in question — as, for instance, in a phrase such as "the Tibetan tradition".

(C) RECOMMENDED READING ON BUDDHISM AND PERENNIALISM

Titus Burckhardt. *Foundations of Oriental Art and Symbolism*, ed. Michael Fitzgerald (Bloomington: World Wisdom, 2007).

Ananda Coomaraswamy. *The Essential Ananda Coomaraswamy*, ed. Rama P. Coomaraswamy (Bloomington: World Wisdom, 2004).

Arnaud Desjardins. *The Message of the Tibetans* (London: Stuart & Watkins, 1969).

Marco Pallis. *Peaks and Lamas* (Berkeley: Counterpoint, 2003).

—. *The Way and the Mountain*, ed. Joseph Fitzgerald (Bloomington: World Wisdom, 2008).

—. *A Buddhist Spectrum* (Bloomington: World Wisdom, 2003).

John Paraskevopoulos. *The Call of the Infinite: the Way of Shin Buddhism* (San Rafael: Sophia Perennis, 2009).

Frithjof Schuon. *Treasures of Buddhism* (Bloomington: World Wisdom, 2018).

—. *Art from the Sacred to the Profane*, ed. Catherine Schuon (Bloomington: World Wisdom, 2007).

Snodgrass, Adrian. *The Symbolism of the Stupa* (Delhi: Motilal Banarsidass, 1992).

Stoddart, William. *An Illustrated Outline of Buddhism* (Bloomington: World Wisdom, 2013).

GLOSSARY OF EASTERN TERMS

(taken largely from World Wisdom publications)

Advaita (Sanskrit): "non-dualist" interpretation of the *Vedānta*; Hindu doctrine according to which the seeming multiplicity of things is regarded as the product of ignorance, the only true reality being *Brahma*, the One, the Absolute, the Infinite, which is the unchanging ground of appearance.

Anattā (Pali): "no self"; the Buddhist doctrine that there is no permanent, unchanging self

Ātmā or **Ātman** (Sanskrit): the real or true "Self", underlying the ego and its manifestations; in the perspective of *Advaita Vedānta*, identical with *Brahma*.

Avatāra (Sanskrit): a divine "descent"; the incarnation or manifestation of God, especially of Vishnu in the Hindu tradition.

Bhakti or **bhakti-mārga** (Sanskrit): the spiritual "path" (*mārga*) of "love" (*bhakti*) and devotion; see *jnāna* and *karma*.

Bodhi (Sanskrit, Pali): "awakened, enlightened"; in Buddhism, the attainment of perfect clarity of mind, in which things are seen as they truly are.

Bodhisattva (Sanskrit, Pali): literally, "enlightenment-being"; in *Mahāyāna* Buddhism, one who postpones his own final enlightenment and entry into *Nirvāna* in order to aid all other sentient beings in their quest for Buddhahood.

Brahma or **Brahman** (Sanskrit): the Supreme Reality, the Absolute.

Dharma (Sanskrit): in Hinduism, the underlying "law" or "order" of the cosmos as expressed in sacred rites and in actions appropriate to various social relationships and human vocations; in Buddhism, the practice and realization of Truth.

Guru (Sanskrit): literally, "weighty", grave, venerable; in Hinduism, a spiritual master; one who gives initiation and instruction in the spiritual path and in whom is embodied the supreme goal of realization or perfection.

Jōdo (Japanese): "pure land"; the untainted, transcendent realm created by the Buddha Amida (Amitabha in Sanskrit), into which his devotees aspire to be born in their next life.

Kali-Yuga (Sanskrit): in Hinduism, the fourth and final *yuga* in a given cycle of time, corresponding to the Iron Age of Western tradition and culminating in a *pralaya* or the *mahāpralaya*; the present age of mankind, distinguished by its increasing disorder, violence, and forgetfulness of God.

Kalpa (Sanskrit): in Hinduism, a "day in the life of Brahmā", understood as lasting one thousand *mahāyugas* or fourteen *manvantaras*.

Karma (Sanskrit): "action, work"; one of the principal *mārgas* or spiritual "paths", characterized by its stress on righteous deeds (see *bhakti* and *jnāna*); in Hinduism and Buddhism, the law of consequence, in which the present is explained by reference to the nature and quality of one's past actions.

Kōan (Japanese): literally, "precedent for public use", case study; in Zen Buddhism, a question or anecdote often based on the experience or sayings of a notable master and involving a paradox or puzzle which cannot be solved in conventional terms or with ordinary thinking.

Mahāyāna (Sanskrit): "great vehicle"; a form of Buddhism, including such traditions as Zen and *Jōdo-Shinshū*, regarded by its followers as the fullest or most adequate expression of the Buddha's teaching; distinguished by the idea that *Nirvāna* is not other than *samsāra* truly seen as it is.

Mahāyuga (Sanskrit): in Hindu tradition, a "great age", comprising four lesser ages (*yugas*) or periods of time, namely, *krita-yuga* (the "golden" age of Western tradition), *tretā-yuga* ("silver"), *dvāpara-yuga* ("bronze"), and *kali-yuga* ("iron").

Mandala (Sanskrit): "circle"; in Hinduism and Buddhism, a symbolic representation of the universe, used in religious ceremonies and meditation.

Mantra (Sanskrit): "instrument of thought"; a word or phrase of divine origin, often including a Name of God, repeated by those initiated into its proper use as a means of salvation or liberation.

Manvantara (Sanskrit): in the Hindu theory of cosmic cycles as derived from the *Mānava-Dharma-Shāstra*, a period of seventy-one *mahāyugas*; see *Yuga*

Māyā (Sanskrit): universal illusion, relativity, appearance; in *Advaita Vedānta*, the veiling or concealment of *Brahma* in the form or under the appearance of a lower, relative reality; also, as "productive power", the unveiling or manifestation of *Ātmā* as "divine art" or theophany. *Māyā* is neither real nor unreal, and ranges from the Supreme Lord to the "last blade of grass".

Moksha (Sanskrit): "release" or "liberation" from *samsāra*; according to Hindu teaching, the most important of the aims of life, attained by following one of the principal *mārgas* or spiritual paths (see *bhakti*, *jnāna*, and *karma*).

Nirvāna (Sanskrit): literally, "blowing out" or "extinction"; in Indian traditions, especially Buddhism, the extinction of suffering and the resulting, blissful state of liberation from egoism and attachment; extinction in relation to universal manifestation.

Samsāra (Sanskrit): literally, "wandering"; in Hinduism and Buddhism, transmigration or the cycle of birth, death, and rebirth; also the world of apparent flux and change.

Satori (Japanese): in Zen Buddhism, the sudden experience of enlightenment; a flash of intuitive insight often gained through the employment of a *kōan* during *zazen* or "sitting meditation".

Shūnyamūrti (Sanskrit): "the form or manifestation of the void"; traditional epithet of the Buddha, in whom is "incarnate" *shūnyatā*, ultimate "emptiness", that is, the final absence of all definite being or selfhood.

Sūtra (Sanskrit): literally, "thread"; a Hindu or Buddhist sacred text; in Hinduism, any short, aphoristic verse or collection of verses, often elliptical in style; in Buddhism, a collection of the discourses of the Buddha.

Tārā (Sanskrit): literally, "she who saves"; the title of a number of Tibetan female *Bodhisattvas* and Hindu goddesses.

Theravāda (Pali): "teaching of the elders"; the oldest surviving school of Buddhism; see *Hīnayāna* and *Mahāyāna*.

Tülku (Tibetan): literally "transformation body"; in Tibetan Buddhism, a person who is recognized at a young age and through various signs as the custodian of a specific lineage of teachings.

Upanishad (Sanskrit): literally, "to sit close by"; hence, any esoteric doctrine requiring direct transmission from master to disciple; in Hinduism, the genre of sacred texts that end or complete the

Vajrayāna (Sanskrit): "diamond vehicle"; a mysterious form of *Mahāyāna* Buddhism prevalent in Tibet emphasizing meditative and tantric practices.

Upāya (Sanskrit): "means, expedient, method"; in Buddhist tradition, the adaptation of spiritual teaching to a form suited to the level of one's audience.

Vedānta (Sanskrit): "end or culmination of the Vedas"; one of the major schools of traditional Hindu philosophy, based in part on the Upanishads, esoteric treatises found at the conclusion of the Vedic scriptures; see *Advaita*

Yoga (Sanskrit): literally, "yoking, union"; in Indian traditions, any meditative and ascetic technique designed to bring the soul and body into a state of concentration.

Yuga (Sanskrit): an "age" in Hinduism, one of the four periods into which a cycle of time is divided.

Zazen (Japanese): literally, "sitting meditation"; in Zen Buddhism, a contemplative practice, often used in conjunction with the *kōan*, and seen as the most direct path to enlightenment.

INDEX

Made in the USA
Monee, IL
29 June 2023

38036432R00144